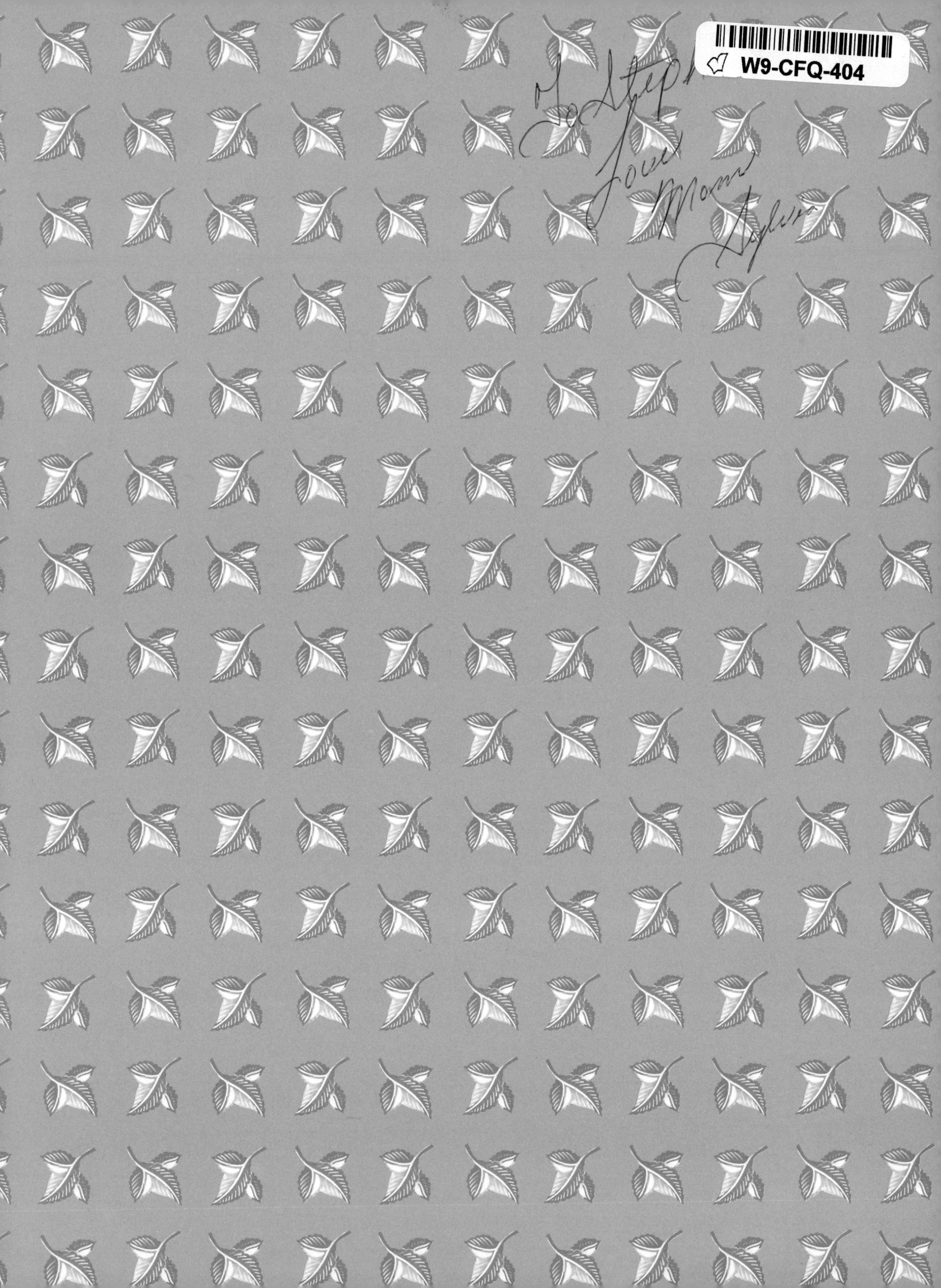

To Steph

love

Mom

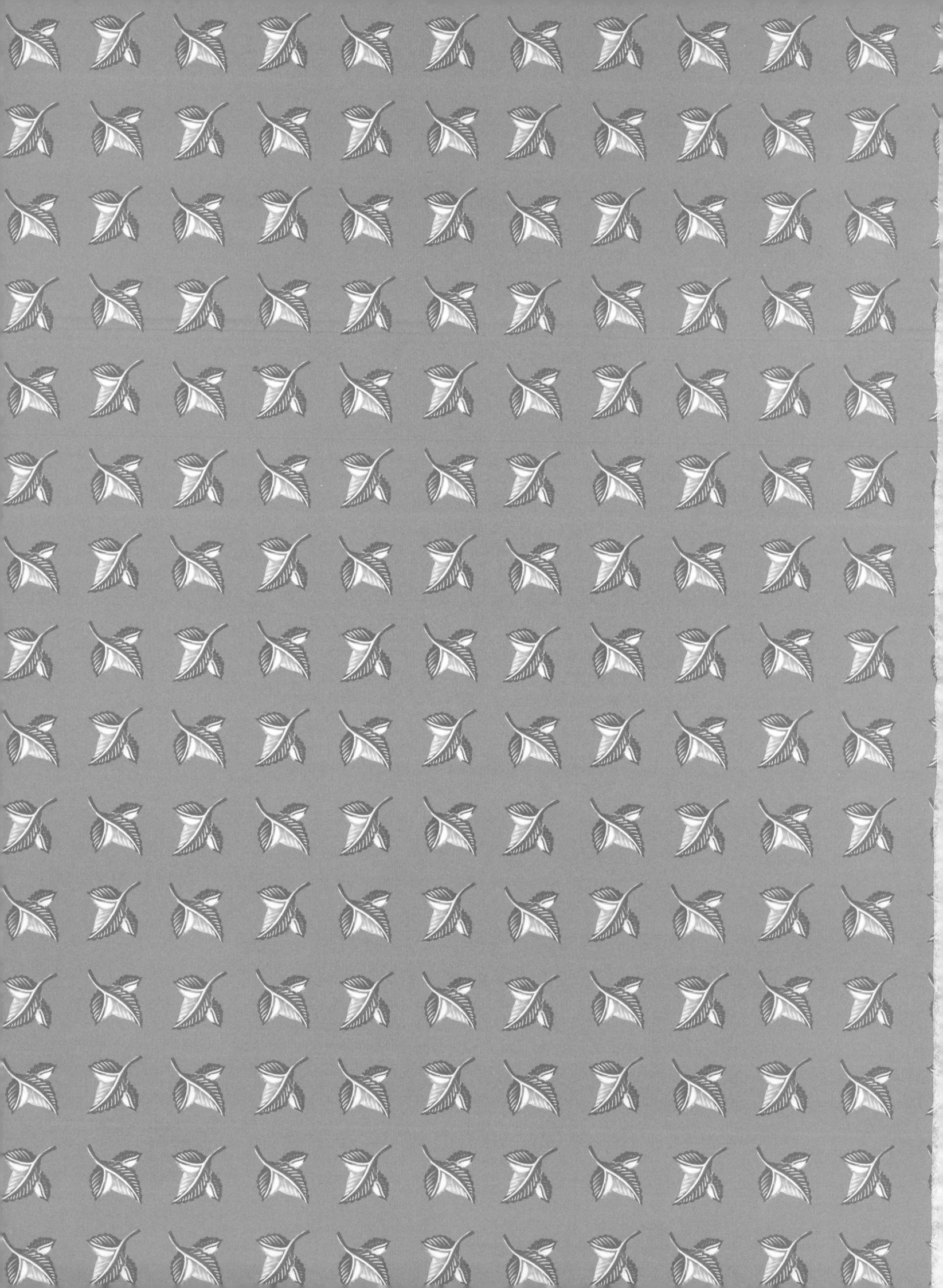

THE COMPLETE
BOOK OF
HERBS

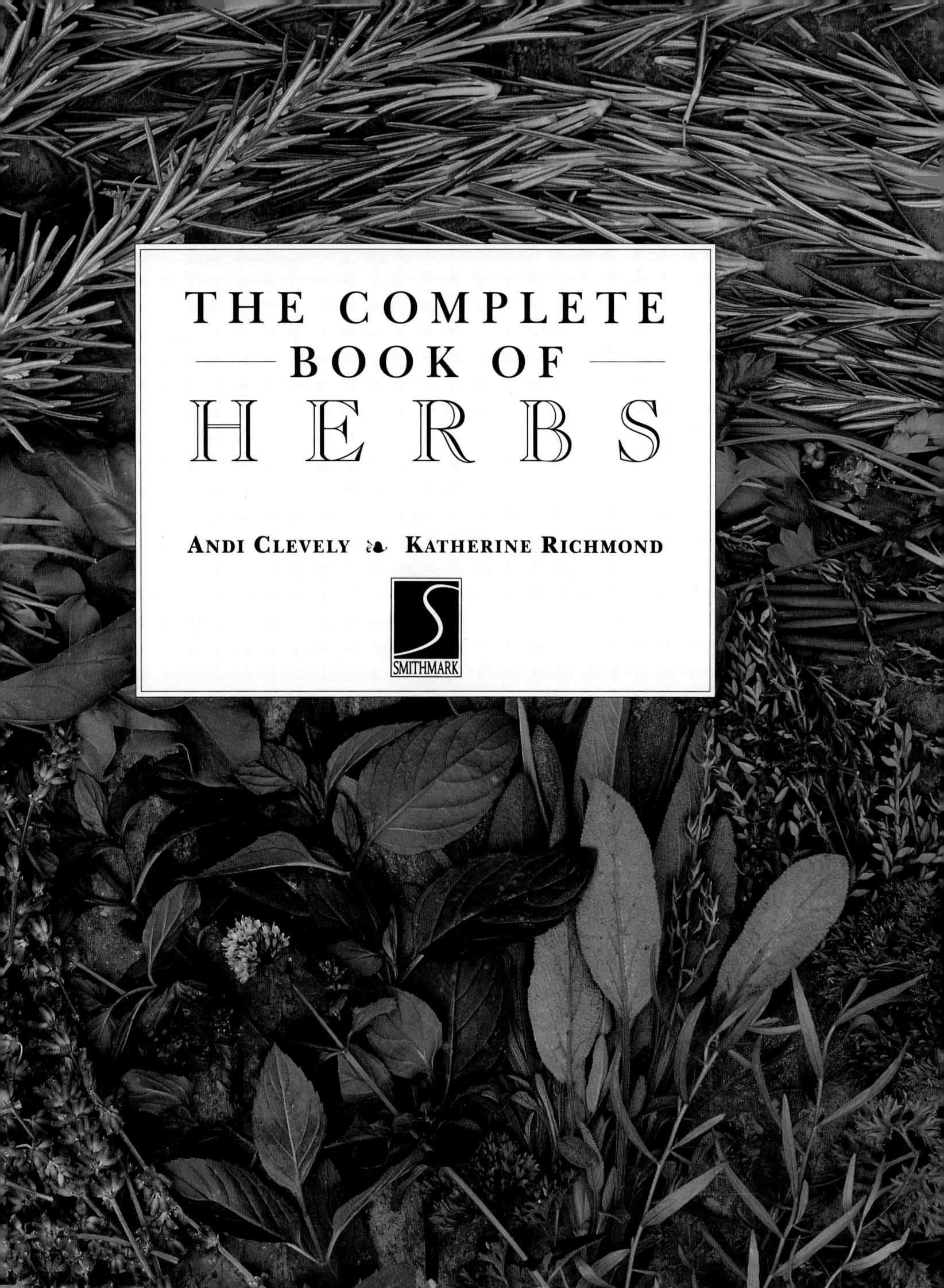

THE COMPLETE
BOOK OF
HERBS

ANDI CLEVELY & KATHERINE RICHMOND

SMITHMARK

Herbs for Healing

Cedronella triphylla

Herbs have long held an important place in the treatment of ailments, and herbal remedies are still popular. Today, the pace of research is accelerating rapidly throughout the world, using various scientific skills to evaluate plants and native traditions in the search for new remedies.

Homer wrote of healing roots, one of the earliest records of the use of medicinal plants in Europe, but Chinese manuals and Indian Ayurvedic texts pre-date this by centuries. Much early herbal medicine was based on superstition: the 'Doctrine of Signatures', for example, stated that a herb would treat that part of the body which it most resembled. European settlers arriving in North America found that the Indian inhabitants had their own version of the doctrine, and would associate yellow herbs with jaundice or red ones with blood disorders.

Most herbal remedies were compounds extracted and blended by apothecaries from several plants, each of which was known on its own as a 'simple'. Apothecaries realized that there were differences in purity and potency between substances found in similar species, and that the effects also depended on factors such as the site where they were gathered, or the time of the month or year. In an attempt to standardize quality, the first secular gardens of simples were established in Pisa, Padua, and thereafter throughout Europe and elsewhere – the first such garden in North America was planted by Dr John Bartram in Philadelphia in 1782. They were organized along the lines of earlier monastic hospital gardens, and were generally known as 'Physic Gardens'. It was here that systematic study of plants began in earnest, combining the disciplines of botany and medicine.

Very often scientific discoveries are based on established local use. Romanies, peasants and rainforest tribesmen alike have needed to be accurate botanists for their very survival. These people have understood the healing capabilities of plants in skilled hands, but they have also appreciated the potential dangers of misuse: rue was chosen by Mohammed, for example, as the most blessed of all herbs and it is central to many Arab and Chinese therapies, but it contains a number of active princi-

Left: *In the herbal pharmacy, fresh or dried herbs have been prepared for medicinal use for centuries, drawing on the accumulated wisdom and experience of generations of herbalists. Diagnosis and prescription are still best left to a qualified practitioner, although simple remedies can be prepared at home.*

HERB BALM

1 A herb balm can soothe aching muscles and so aid relaxation. Weigh out 1 oz fresh lavender and rosemary stems, mixed.

2 Place the herbs in a small pan set over a bain-marie. Add 1 pint olive or sunflower oil. Cover with a light lid and simmer for 2 hours, adding more water as necessary.

3 Allow to cool slightly then strain the liquid into a clean bowl.

4 Leave the liquid to cool and then pour into a sterilized jar or bottle and seal. Apply sparingly.

ples which often cause sensitivity to light, and people often develop skin rashes after contact with the plant.

Herbs interact in complex ways with our body chemistry, and their power to heal is formidable. Compared with synthetic drugs their actions may seem very mild, but you should not underestimate the dangers of self-medication on the assumption that herbs are harmless. Many traditional remedies are based on fantasy, guesswork and suggestion, while even the most reputable herbs are selective in their effects, working for one patient but not another.

Only a trained practitioner is qualified to diagnose an ailment, and then to suggest a personal prescription after fully assessing your individual needs. The medical benefits of herbs are no longer in doubt, and many are generally quite safe, provided that they are not misused or taken in circumstances

Right: *It is not just the visible flowers and leaves of herbs that are valuable. Very often the fresh or dried roots, such as those of comfrey, contain the highest concentrations of active ingredients.*

where allergic reactions or side effects are possible – even garlic, widely regarded as an infallible panacea, may reduce blood pressure and so cancel the impact of drugs taken for cardiac disorders. All the plants are complex factories producing diverse chemicals, some of them fragrances to attract pollinating insects, others toxins to deter predators, and any one of these substances may be harmful in particular circumstances.

NATURAL INSECTICIDES

Many plants produce natural insecticides as part of their defence systems, and some of these are widely used as prepared powders and liquids in the garden. Derris, or rotenone, a popular insecticide approved for organic use, is extracted from the powdered roots of a Malaysian shrub known as tuba root (*Derris elliptica*).

Sometimes particular species are grown as companion plants to protect crops nearby from attack.

Various *Tagetes* species have been found to repel whitefly and other pests when grown in greenhouses, and scientific experiments now confirm that their flowers emit volatile chemicals into the surrounding air for protection. As these have proved toxic to the mosquitoes that carry malaria and yellow fever, it is hoped that a new generation of insecticides can be developed for their control.

Herbs for Dyeing

Anyone who has gathered wild blackberries in autumn or pinched out sideshoots from tomato plants will readily appreciate the possibilities of using plant stains to dye animal skins and woven material. Until chemical dyes were introduced, roots, bark, flowers and leaves were the chief sources of color, often made permanent by the addition of mordants – fixing chemicals – from mineral-rich earths and other sources. The shades obtained are rarely vivid, but mellow, subtle, and full of the lustrous beauty of the plants themselves.

Urtica divica

Ancient China, India and other Asian countries developed sophisticated skills in dyeing, but similar techniques have always been used by tribespeople around the world, who adapted plant materials for painting on bark, to ornament clothing or decorate the skin in preparation for religious ceremonies or warfare, and even for disguise – Romanies once artificially tanned their faces with juices obtained from a favorite herb, *Lycopus europaeus* or gipsywort. The early Britons were described by Julius Caesar as 'blue and terrible' after they had dyed their skin with woad to make their appearance more alarming, while in ancient Egypt the plant was also used to color imperial garments.

Dyeing with herbs remains a popular and pleasant craft, although large amounts of material are often needed, and colors tend to fade gently unless made fast with chemical mordants such as alum, tin, iron or chrome. Results vary according to the strength of the dye, the length of time that the wool (the easiest material to color) is left immersed, and the parts of a plant that are used: the leaves of privet, for example, give yellow shades, whereas the berries impart a muted blue-green hue.

Some plants can be gathered from the wild, but in view of the amounts needed there is the risk of over-

Above: *Woad, or dyer's rocket, is cultivated in many countries for its distinctive blue dye.*

Left: *Manufacture of indigo dye paste from a species of* Indigofera *in south-west China.*

harvesting species that may not be abundant, and it is often better to grow your own supplies of the more useful kinds in a special dye border. This can be an attractive feature, for many of the plants are popular garden ornamentals whose flowers or fruits are the parts used, so that geraniums, dahlias, rudbeckia and mulberries can earn a place as dye plants in the herb garden. Experiment with various leaves after pruning or clipping shrubs and hedges, as many will impart various shades of yellow and green.

CLASSIC DYE CROPS

Traditional dye plants worth growing include the ancient woad (*Isatis tinctoria*), a leafy spinach-like plant whose use dwindled rapidly after the introduction of the more permanent blue dye from the indigo plant, *Indigofera tinctoria*, a subtropical species which needs to be grown in a warm greenhouse in temperate regions.

Dyer's madder (*Rubia tinctorum*) is a self-seeding perennial still cultivated

Above: *Woolen yarn dyed using homegrown* Polygonum tinctorum. *Shades are varied by the number of immersions in the vat.*

Right: *Indigo plants,* Strobilanthes flaccidifolius, *growing in a field in Guizhou Province, south-west China. Plants are cultivated annually from cuttings – the precursor of the dye is contained in the leaves.*

on a field scale in France and the Netherlands, and an important European source of strong red, while in North America bloodroot (*Sanguinaria canadensis*) was the main plant used by Indians for red body paint. Weld (*Reseda luteola*) (or dyer's greenweed, *Genista tinctoria*), a relative of broom, another dye source, is a traditional yellow dye plant with handsome flower spikes, and a tendency to colonize unless seedlings are kept in check.

The elder is guardian of all herbs according to folklore, and planting one of these will provide you with a green dye from the leaves and, from the berries, lilac (using alum mordant) or purple (using chrome).

SELECTED PLANTS FOR A DYE GARDEN

Part of the creative adventure of dyeing with plants is that the shades obtained can be varied considerably by using different mordants, so that madder, for example, can produce anything from light pink to dark brown.

- reds, pinks: bloodroot, chenopodium, madder, pokeberry, rose hips, sorrel
- yellows and orange: beetroot, coreopsis, dahlias, golden rod, heather, marigolds, Osage orange, pear leaves, rudbeckia, saffron, turmeric, weld, zinnias
- black: meadowsweet, walnut
- blues: blackberries, blueberries, dandelion root, elderberries, indigo, juniper berries, woad, yellow flag

- greens: bracken, dock, lily of the valley, nettles, weld
- browns: gipsywort, madder, sassafras, sumac, various barks (apple, birch, walnut), willow

Choosing Sites for Herbs

Thymus vulgaris

Choosing a suitable site for a herb needs preliminary assessment of factors such as the type of plant, the soil, the aspect, the exposure and the local temperature range. There are also practical considerations of space and appearance in relation to the rest of the garden. All this needs careful thought before starting to plant up sites.

Every form of gardening is artificial and depends for its success on matching as far as possible the natural environment of the plants. Herbs that you intend cultivating will be assembled in one place, and yet they come originally from all parts of the world and every kind of soil and climate.

Always find out where your herbs normally grow in the wild – it might be a sun-baked rocky hillside near the Mediterranean Sea or a well-watered rainforest where frost is unknown, a cool temperate woodland, or cold exposed cliff where wind keeps growth short and compact. Try to identify the warmest sheltered parts of the garden, the areas with the best drainage or dappled shade, corners where frost lingers or the sun arrives first in the morning, and allocate herbs according to their preferences. If you are planning a separate herb garden, assess its position at all times of the year and from all cultural aspects, and then choose the plants

Below: *A general mixed bed of herbs, combining, for example, borage, comfrey, lovage and lavender: this looks very effective against a backdrop of traditional wattle fencing.*

PLANNING A SMALL BORDER

Herbs for the back layer – 3 ft upwards
* perennials: angelica, artemisia, bergamot, elecampane, fennel, liquorice, lovage, meadowsweet, rosemary, sea holly, shrub roses, European or American sweet cicely
* annuals and biennials: alexanders, foxglove, mullein

Herbs for the middle section – 1 ft 6 in-3 ft
* perennials: agrimony, balm, chicory, comfrey, costmary, curry plant, lavender, rampion, rue, sage, santolina, southernwood, St John's wort, tansy, tarragon, valerian, white horehound
* annuals and biennials: borage, bugloss, caraway, dill

Herbs for the front edge – up to 1 ft 6 in
* perennials: bistort, calamint, catmint, chamomile, chives, herb bennet, hyssop, lady's smock, marjoram, mint, sedum, sorrel, thyme, winter savory, wormwood, yarrow
* annuals and biennials: anise, basil, chervil, clary, coriander, cumin, marigold, parsley, summer savory

that are most likely to succeed in its various beds.

Remember that the term 'herbs' is used as a broad and imprecise classification, and includes plants with very different life cycles. Annuals and biennials are short-term plants, the former completing their growth from germination to shedding seed within a single season (some such as chervil can manage more than one generation per year). This partly determines where they are grown, for they will change rapidly in appearance and leave gaps in a planting scheme when they have died down. Biennials germinate and make leafy growth during their first season, survive the winter on the stored nutrients in their roots, and then flower and set seed the following year; if they are grown for their foliage, you can treat them as annuals, but for flower and seed crops they will need space for two years.

Perennials, which may be hardy or tender according to their origin, provide the framework of any herb garden design, for they are permanent and maintain continuity from one year to the next.

Size varies widely, with some herbs low-growing but liable to expand sideways into broad ground-hugging mats of foliage, while others are tall and dominating. Ultimate height and spread should always be taken into account when planning beds and herb gardens, together with a plant's tolerance of pruning and clipping, for many bulky subjects such as evergreen shrubs can be cut back to manageable size. Site plants of various heights according to their probable impact on an overall design: the tallest species work best in the center of island beds viewed from all sides or at the back of borders, with the shortest plants at the

PLANTING A HEDGE

1 Mark out and excavate a shallow trench running the length of the proposed hedge, and thoroughly fork over the soil in the bottom to ensure good drainage.

2 Hedging plants need plenty of nourishment in their early years, so add a generous amount of garden compost to the trench and lightly fork in.

3 Mark the center line of the hedge with string and pegs, and space out the plants, using a length of cane or wooden batten to measure equal distances between them.

4 Planted, firmed and watered in the refilled trench, the hedge will soon begin to fill out, ready for its first trim to shape.

front, although positioning a large, attractive specimen where it is least expected (within a sea of contrasting short plants, perhaps, or on a bend in a path to conceal an alcove) can produce a satisfying impact.

Growing herbs in containers is the ideal solution where considerations of space, soil or climate suggest a plant might be difficult to grow. This is not a poor substitute for open-ground cultivation, but an attractive branch of gardening in its own right. Most herbs

adapt to pots and other containers, and when well tended can create satisfying collections to enhance otherwise barren areas of the garden – courtyards, flights of steps, entrances and exits, for example – and make herb growing a practical choice for window boxes, balconies and roof gardens. It is easy to supply container-grown plants with the kind of soil they prefer, and to move them under cover or to sunny spots if they are sensitive to cold or exposure.

Above: *Raised beds built within stone walls are convenient sites for herbs such as rosemary. They offer good drainage and ease of picking.*

Above: *Shady woodland spots suit many herbs which do not tolerate direct sun and dry soil. Herbs such as peppermint may provide useful ground cover for barer patches beneath trees in cultivated gardens.*

Planning the Herb Garden

Formal or relaxed, utilitarian or decorative, a herb garden must be satisfying to look at and work in, and manageable in terms of your time, needs, energy and commitment. A complex parterre, for example, must be kept clipped, weed-free and carefully aligned for success, whereas the cottage garden approach of profusion without confusion may be more appropriate if you want plentiful supplies of useful herbs combined with cheerful diversity and low maintenance.

Levisticum officinale

Once you have explored the potential site and the chances of your chosen herbs liking the position, there is style to consider. This is an intangible but important matter, taking into account not only your personal tastes but the nature of the site, for any garden or border is intimately bonded to the house, and to the immediate and distant surroundings.

With a fairly clear vision of the garden you would like, you can draw together all the various elements in a final design. Measure the garden or plot, and mark its outline on graph

Above: *Design herb beds and borders to take advantage of contrasts between colors and shapes, but remember to match for height and impact.*

paper, together with existing assets such as shrubs and paths that are to be retained, and important nearby features – fences or hedges, large trees that might cast shade, and the house itself. Mark in with symbols the essential bones of the scheme, the new paths and beds, large plants, watercourses. The smaller the intended garden, the easier this planning stage will be, and for a simple bed of culinary herbs you might be able to omit drawing up a design altogether.

For larger plans always beware the illusion that you have more room in the garden than actually exists: it is easy on paper to draw a path or pack a large number of herbs into a given space, and then find that the result is hopelessly cramped or out of scale, or has unexpected visual effects on the rest of the garden. Look up the likely spread of trees and shrubs, mark this precisely on the plan, and then check frequently with the site itself; if necessary position stakes where significant plants and features are to go, or lay a garden hose on the ground to assess

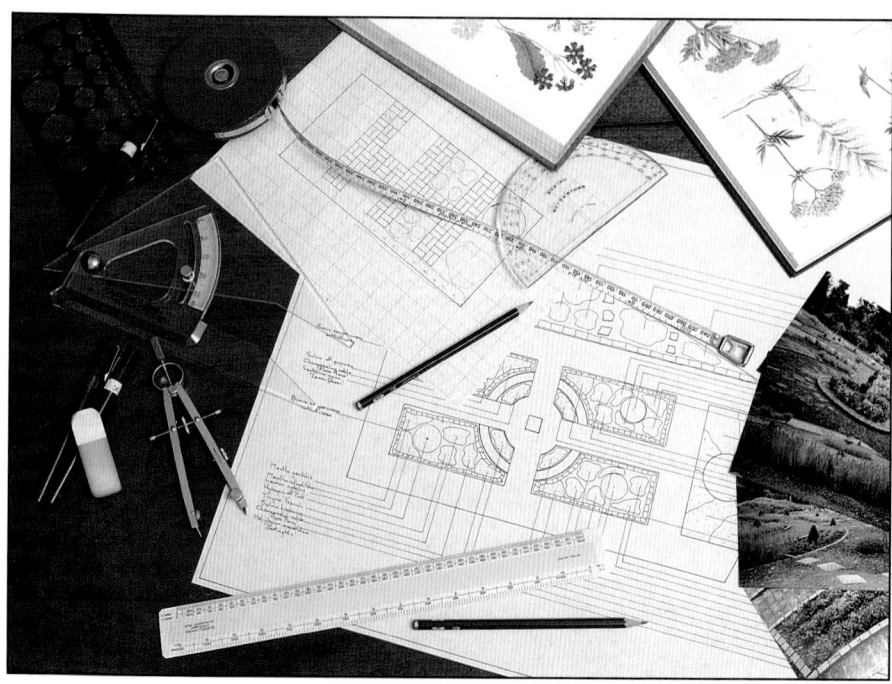

Left: *Avoid mistakes and disappointment by making careful preliminary plans, drawing out the proposed design to scale to check its impact and feasibility.*

LAYING A PATH

1 Mark out and excavate the path, arranging stout boards along the sides with their upper edges at the finished surface level. Spread and compact a foundation of hardcore such as stones or broken brick.

2 Cover the base with a bed of sand, lightly tamped with the head of a rake to fill any gaps in the hardcore, and then rake a loose level surface in which to bed the bricks.

3 Arrange the bricks on the widest side in an attractive bond or pattern, firming them into place with the handle of a hammer and checking the surface in all directions with a spirit level as you go.

4 With all the bricks set out, spread more sand over the surface and brush repeatedly to fill all the joints; clear away any surplus sand.

5 Ease sand from the joints with a knife to create pockets for prostrate herbs which may be sown directly or, as here, planted as divisions from established specimens.

6 Tuck a little compost around the plants, firm into place and water if necessary; they will soon spread into mats and cushions of fragrant foliage.

the shape and course of a path or bed.

Work out planting schemes for individual beds and borders on separate sheets of paper only when you are satisfied with all this preliminary work make any necessary basic adjustments after trying out possible variations on the ground.

In addition to pictorial plans, you should also draw up a schedule of the work involved, because the various tasks are often best done in a particular order, perhaps at certain times of the year to ensure the least amount of disorder, mess and delay. Planting itself is almost the final operation and best timed for autumn in mild areas, or spring where winters are severe.

Before then you will need to repair or renovate existing hard structures such as paths, fences and walls, prune or move plants at the appropriate season, and remove turf or weeds to leave a clear site for marking out. Separate smaller beds can be prepared and planted piecemeal, but when planning a complete herb garden it is best to complete all these preliminary stages before transferring your design to the ground, using pegs driven in securely and joined with strings to mark the basic outlines. You can then dig over beds and borders to a suitable depth and condition, and set about constructing paths and hard edges.

Plant Requirements

Consideration should be given to the requirements of individual herbs for successful growth and yield; different surroundings are suitable for different herbs and a little time spent researching the ideal environment will help to produce a wonderful crop of pungent and decorative plants.

Lavandula spica

Although most of the well-known herbs are of Mediterranean origin and therefore prefer a sunny, free-draining position, re-creating the ecology they evolved in does not mean aiming deliberately for impoverished conditions. Only the nasturtium is recommended for hungry sites, because these encourage the production of flowers that might otherwise be usurped by lush leaf growth; but the result of improved flowering in the case of the nasturtium is often early death. It is worth remembering that most plants grown in gardens are often superior in form, size and performance to their relatives in the wild: the fact that they have adapted naturally

to spartan surroundings is no reason to deny them care and nourishment.

It is fair to say, though, that aromatic herbs grown for flavoring or medicinal use are best grown in full sun, whereas those grown as pot herbs and leaf crops prefer moister conditions and some shelter from hot sunshine if they are to make plenty of growth. Arrange beds or the distribution of plants within a herb garden according to these needs, assembling leafy plants, for example, at the shady end of a border, in the shadow of shrubs, near hedges or beneath the canopy of open-pruned trees to provide them with a little dappled shade. Remember that variegated plants

yield their best colors when exposed to morning and evening sunlight with a little shade at midday.

Similarly, free drainage is important for plants that are intolerant of damp conditions. These include plants with silver and grey foliage, which is usually produced by dense fine leaf hairs intended to trap moisture, developed as an adaptation to very dry conditions. Other plants of dubious hardiness may also succumb to prolonged damp around the stems. Raised beds or gravel mulches around stem bases can sometimes improve their chances of survival. Most woody-stemmed perennials need plenty of warm sunlight to ripen their growth and ensure

DIVIDING A BED

1 Segregate herbs with underground runners from other, more vulnerable plants with wide slates or pieces of durable paneling inserted vertically.

2 Replace the soil on both sides of the division, and firm into place with your heel or the handle of a trowel.

3 An invasive herb such as mint can then be planted a little distance from the inconspicuous division.

that they are well prepared to withstand winter temperatures.

Herbs that like damp, partially shaded sites, on the other hand, only thrive where their needs are met, both hot dry soil and gloomy waterlogged positions proving intolerable to them. Herbaceous perennial herbs, in particular, need to make maximum growth during the growing season to stock their roots with enough nutrients for survival and re-emergence the following spring.

Most herbs need shelter of some kind from the extremes of wind and frost. Though they might survive in the wild, their growth is often stunted by wind-pruning and frost injury, and you will do them a favor by enclosing beds and borders with windbreak hedges or fences that reduce their exposure. You will reap the benefits in summer, when the still sheltered air is heavy with the concentrated fragrance of volatile oils. Make sure, however, that the garden is not so enclosed that it becomes a frost pocket, without gateways or openings for cold air to drain away from susceptible plants.

SLOPING GROUND

Level ground is not essential unless you are planning an impressive parterre or knot garden, which really needs construction on a prepared platform in the same way as a bowling green or formal lawn. For most other herb schemes sloping ground, especially a dry bank, is ideal as a means of guaranteeing good drainage and, if it faces the sun for a large part of the day, plenty of warmth and light. There are enough prostrate and trailing herb varieties to ensure adequate ground cover and protection against soil erosion on a bank, but for larger specimens or where the incline is very steep,

making simple terraces or small level planting pockets will help with rapid establishment and any watering needed until plants are self-reliant. Paths can be cut as a series of steps, their outline perhaps softened by cascading thymes, ground-hugging Corsican mint, or tufts of chamomile and the creeping savory *Satureja spicigera*.

Above: *Herbs that need warm conditions do well when planted along the base of a brick wall facing the sun, which remains warm even after nightfall.*

Right: *A simple pit surrounded with firm walls of bricks or old wooden beams provides a useful bed for larger herbs, or (as here) a propagation and nursery frame that can be covered in cold weather.*

Above: *Stepping stones made from sawn log sections or paving slabs are a simple means of providing access for planting and maintenance in larger beds, and soon merge with the herbs as these grow and spread.*

HERBS FOR HEAVY SOILS

Although wet clays and other intractable soils will always benefit from some improvement to open their texture and speed drainage, the following herbs can usually cope well, especially if the surface is mulched in summer to prevent drought and cracking. Sunny or shaded sites are suitable, except where stated otherwise.

• alexanders	• angelica
• borage (sun)	• calendula
• chives (sun)	• comfrey
• fennel (sun)	• lemon balm (sun)
• lovage	• mint
• nasturtium (sun)	• sage
• sorrel	• sweet cicely

Structuring the Herb Garden

The design of a formal herb garden, whether it is a complex of knots or a simple wheel with radiating spokes dividing beds of culinary plants, allows plenty of scope for imagination. As William Lawson wrote in the seventeenth century, 'For special forms in squares, there are as many as there are devices in Gardeners' brains.' Simplicity is essential, for an elaborate layout will merely look confused once plants start to grow, and will only be comprehensible if viewed from above.

Gratiola officinalis

Graph paper is essential, as are accurate measurements. Sketch in the outlines of beds and borders as a rough guide, by all means, but decide first on the layout and dimensions of paths. Ornament is one thing, access at all seasons for harvesting and tending plants another, and all paths should be wide enough for comfortable passage (especially between shrubs after heavy rain) and must reach all parts of the garden. Main paths should be at least 2 ft wide, more if you use a wheelbarrow or need wheelchair access. You can make subsidiary paths narrower – 12 in might be enough – or you could use stepping stones instead of a continuous surface. Position the odd slab in large beds to stand on, or limit the beds' width to about 4 ft so that all herbs are within arm's reach.

While balance and good proportion are important in planning the layout of beds, there is no reason why an irregular herb garden cannot be as successful as a classically symmetrical one. Draw out several geometrical patterns of beds on tracing paper laid over the garden outline drawn to scale on squared paper, and check their measurements for practicality. Leave room for seats, statuary and other features, and remember that hedges occupy substantial space – allow a 12 in width for dwarf hedges, more for taller ones.

A series of small beds, each planted with a single type of herb, provides simple bold blocks of color and texture, but more comprehensive plant collections need larger beds, perhaps organized according to color, height or use. With elaborate designs, always measure the diagonals to make sure they are truly symmetrical, and take all measurements accurately, starting where possible from a base line – that is, the longest straight line that can be measured on the site – which can be used as a reference for all other

Left: *Herbs adapt to a number of styles and designs, not least to a relaxed cottage garden arrangement where the plants can grow and flower with their natural informality.*

A-Z of Herbs

Achillea millefolium (Compositae)
Yarrow

milfoil, nosebleed, herb militaris, soldier's woundwort, thousand leaf, thousand seal, field hop

Description: hardy herbaceous pungent perennial, 6-24 in. Finely feathered, bright gray-green leaves and flat heads of small white, pink or red flowers midsummer to autumn. Grows in grassy places, including lawns.

Use: folk remedy for rheumatism, toothache, hemorrhage and fever; fresh young leaves used sparingly in salads; herbal tobacco and substitute for hops in brewing.

Cultivation: prefers full sun and well-drained ground; good for chalky and seaside gardens. Spreads readily, so segregate from other plants. Divide roots in spring or autumn, or sow seeds from spring until autumn; plant 6 in apart for lawns.

Parts used: top growth cut just before flowering. Dry outdoors in the shade or in gentle heat indoors.

Related species: *A. decolorans* (English mace): half-hardy perennial, 18-24 in, native to southern Europe. Feathery leaves; yellow flowers, summer. Light soil in full sun.

A. moschata (musk yarrow): rhizomatous perennial, 8 in, from European Alps. Ferny leaves; white flowers, summer. Needs good drain-age and full sun.

Agrimonia eupatoria (Rosaceae)
Common Agrimony

church steeples, liverwort, sticklewort, cockleburr

Description: wayside perennial often found on chalk, 6 in-2 ft. Attractive gray-green cinquefoil leaves, arranged in alternate large and small pairs, with pale yellow star-shaped flowers in summer on tapering spikes like a mullein; apricot scent, popular with bees. Seedheads are burrs which stick to clothes and fur.

Use: once regarded as a magic herb for healing jaundice; used as a spring tonic, as an astringent externally for treating wounds, and in oriental medicine to stop bleeding; a valuable yellow dye plant.

Cultivation: likes well-drained soil in full sun, but will also thrive in short grass. Sow in a seedbed outdoors in spring or autumn, or divide established roots in autumn.

Parts used: whole plant for dyeing; fresh leaves steeped in water to make an infusion; aerial parts except thick stems may be gathered just before flowering for drying gently in the dark; roots may be dried and grated to add to pot-pourri.

Related species: *A. odorata* (fragrant agrimony): highly aromatic plant with sticky, hairy leaves, larger in all parts than *A. eupatoria*. Often planted in wild and woodland gardens.

Ajuga reptans (Labiatae)
Common Bugle

creeping bugle, carpet bugle, carpenter's herb (note that North American bugle, bugleweed or gipsy wort refers to *Lycopus* spp.)

Description: short prostrate perennial, 6 in. Rosettes of coarse shining green leaves, and spires of blue, white or rose flowers in midsummer. Spreads freely by runners. Several cultivated forms including 'Atropurpurea', with metallic purple leaves, and 'Variegata', cream and green, grows best in shade.

Use: medicinally to treat bleeding from cuts and other wounds; popular ground cover among other herbs and for edging containers.

Cultivation: grows in moist, rich soils in shade or full sun; flourishes beneath hedges if compost is added. Sow in spring or autumn in trays and barely cover seed – germination is slow and erratic. Separate established roots and transplant divisions in spring or autumn.

Parts used: leaves picked as required and simmered to make an infusion; whole herb cut down to ground level in summer and dried in shade.

Related species: *A. chamaepitys* (ground-pine, arthritic ivy): short bushy annual with pine scent, 4-6 in. Red-spotted yellow flowers in summer. Whole herb used to treat bleeding and high pulse rate, and in Arab veterinary treatments.

Alchemilla vulgaris (Rosaceae)

Common Lady's Mantle

lion's foot, bear's foot, common alchemil

Description: an aggregate of closely related species, typically herbaceous perennials, 6-18 in. Leaves cloak-shaped and pleated. Small yellowish-green flowers in summer.

Use: used by alchemists in attempts to make gold; folk remedy for eye disorders and to stop bleeding; traditional treatment for menstrual disorders and in childbirth.

Cultivation: grows in sun or shade, in walls, as edging and as ground cover under trees and shrubs, where it self-seeds freely. Sow in trays in summer, and plant out in autumn; or divide clumps in early spring or autumn.

Parts used: leaves and flower shoots picked as required; aerial parts gathered in summer and dried outdoors.

Related species: *A. alpina* (alpine lady's mantle): evergreen dwarf perennial, grows to 8 in, for sinks, rock gardens and short grass in sun; soft furry, silvery leaves, tiny yellow flowers.

A. arvensis (parsley piert, field lady's mantle): similar to *A. vulgaris*, popular Romany tonic and remedy for bladder stone.

Allium (Liliaceae)

The various species all possess the familiar sulphurous smell, but individually they are valued as vegetables, herbs, medicines and decorative garden bulbs. Only the most important in herbal terms are described here.
Caution: some people are slightly allergic to all forms of onions.

Allium sativum

Garlic

Description: subterranean white-skinned bulb, subdivided into numerous 'cloves'. Short, flat upright leaves, 6-12 in, tall single flower stem bearing spherical head of pale pink or greenish-white blooms often mixed with tiny bulbils.

Uses: flavoring, vegetable and medicinal herb that has accumulated superstitions over the centuries. Used as an antibiotic, expectorant and digestive, and for treating high blood pressure.

Cultivation: cloves planted in autumn 2-4 in deep in rich soil, or in pots in a frame for planting out in spring in cold regions. Harvested in summer when foliage dies down, and dried in sunlight or warmth.

Parts used: bulbs, separated into cloves.

Related species: *A. oleraceum* (field garlic, wild garlic), *A. triquetrum* (three-cornered garlic), *A. scorodoprasum* (sand leek) and *A. rosea* (rosy garlic) used in various parts of the world as wild substitutes for garlic.

A. ursinum (wild garlic, ramsons): white-flowered wild onion, widespread in damp woodland; pungent garlic smell, but mild when cooked.

A. vineale (wild garlic, crow garlic): wiry version of cultivated garlic, widespread in temperate regions. Used by North American Indians.

Allium schoenoprasum

Chives

Description: small perennial bulb growing in clumps, with fine hollow dark green leaves, 8-12 in, and slightly taller flower stems bearing small clusters of mauve or purple blooms. Can be found wild in moist soils, but usually cultivated.

chives

Uses: mainly culinary for flavoring and garnishing where a mild onion flavor is required. Also a stimulant and digestive; high in vitamin C. Popular decorative herb for edging and for attracting bees. Chive tea is sometimes sprayed to prevent gooseberry mildew and apple scab. Chive flowers can be used in decorative dried flower arrangements.

Cultivation: sow seeds outdoors in spring, or divide clumps into small groups and plant in spring or autumn in moist rich soil. Lift and divide every 3-5 years according to growth. May be potted up in autumn for forcing winter supplies indoors.

(Continued)

Parts used: fresh leaves cut as needed. Chop and freeze in bags or ice-cube trays for use out of season.

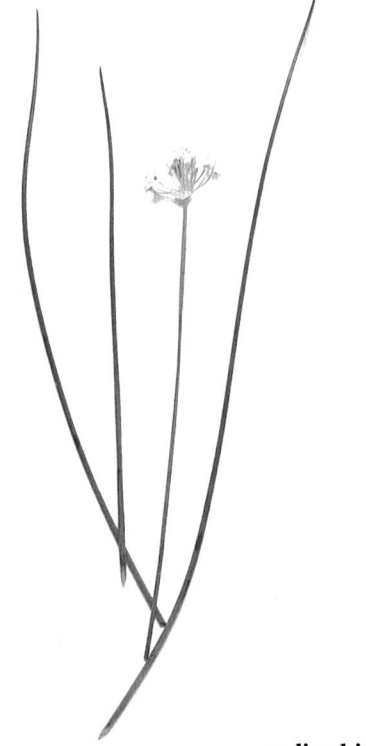

garlic chive

Related species: Larger-leaved forms available; also Chinese or garlic chives (*A. tuberosum*) and Siberian chives (*A. schoenoprasum sibiricum*).

Aloe vera, syn. *A. barbadensis* (Liliaceae)

❧ Aloes

Cape aloes, socotrine, medicine plant, burn plant

Description: succulent drought-resistant tropical plant forming clumps of short-stemmed rosettes of fleshy evergreen leaves, up to 2 ft long, pointed and edged with teeth. Tall flower stem with spikes of yellow, orange or red tubular blooms. Often grown as a house plant in cool regions.

Uses: according to legend the sole survivor from the Garden of Eden. Gel-like sap from leaves used externally to heal wounds, burns and mastitis. **Caution:** traditional internal use as purgative bitters ill advised and may cause hemorrhage.

Cultivation: plants need sunny, arid conditions. May be started from seed in spring, or propagated from small offsets at base of parent plant. As house plants, best grown in gritty cactus mixtures in good light; minimum winter temperature of 41°F to ensure flowering, in summer may be stood outdoors. In frost-free gardens, ideal plants for sunny beds with fast drainage.

Parts used: broken leaves rubbed on affected part. Sap extracted from leaves and often dried to form a resin.

Related species: *A. aristata*: small relative with leaves 4-6 in long, white spines and orange flowers. Popular house plant and hardiest of the tropical aloes; may survive mild temperate winters out of doors.

Althaea officinalis (Malvaceae)

❧ **Marsh Mallow**

guimauve, mortification plant, schloss tea, sweet weed, wymote

Description: tough-rooted herbaceous perennial, 4 ft. Velvety stems and leaves; white or pink flowers in leaf axils in late summer. Found in damp, often saline places.

Uses: valuable and handsome herb with a long tradition of use in medicine and cosmetics, and as a vegetable and confection. Cultivated by the Romans and promoted by Charlemagne. Soothing and mucilaginous; tops of young shoots added to salads (popular with Bedu); flowers and leaves infused to treat lung and bowel disorders; roots sliced and boiled to poultice external inflammation and relieve gastric ailments; root was made into traditional 'marshmallows' (now just sugar and gelatin).

Cultivation: sow seeds in spring indoors in warmth, or outdoors in summer, and transplant to permanent positions in autumn. Roots may be divided in spring or autumn. On light soils mulch freely in summer.

Parts used: flowers, leaves and young tips of shoots gathered fresh; roots at least 2 years old, dug up during winter dormancy when the active constituents are most concentrated, and used fresh or dried.

Althaea Rosea
🐾 **Hollyhock**

Description: biennial or perennial of waste places, and traditional cottage garden flower; grows up to 10 ft. Wide hairy leaves, up to 12 in across. Large flowers, often double, in summer; wild forms are white or pink; cultivated forms purple, red or yellow.

Uses: petals of purple-flowered variety once used to dye wine. Leaves used medicinally as a diuretic and to help some chest complaints. Provides relief for mouth ulcers; soothing to the face.

Cultivation: can be grown in any soil. Propagate from seed and prick out.

Parts used: flowers and leaves, fresh.

Anethum graveolens
(Umbelliferae)
🐾 **Dill**
dillseed, dillweed

Description: annual herb, 18-30 in, with finely feathered blue-green leaves and hollow stems. Small open umbels of creamy-yellow flowers in summer, followed by dark brown seeds. Grows wild in waste places, but can also be cultivated.

Uses: used as a condiment and flavoring and as a pickling spice. Often taken as 'dill water' to relieve digestive problems and flatulence. Occasionally used to perfume cosmetics; medicinal oil distilled from leaves, stems and seeds.

Cultivation: sow in rows or small patches in spring, and again in early summer for continuity, in a sunny, well-drained position. Grow well away from fennel, with which dill cross-pollinates readily. Choose right variety for seed or leaf production.

Parts used: young leaves gathered at any time for use fresh, also flowers for adding to soups; seeds harvested when dry for use whole or crushed. Leaves may be dried, but lose much of their flavor.

Related species: *A. sowa* (Indian dill, Japanese dill): similar in appearance and uses, popular in Asian cuisines.

Angelica archangelica
(Umbelliferae)
🐾 **Angelica**
garden angelica, Holy Ghost

Description: a robust biennial or short-lived perennial plant, 6 ft, of damp woodlands. Produces a few large, deeply indented leaves at ground level, followed by tall hollow stems bearing from their leaf sheaths heads of greenish-white flowers in midsummer.

Uses: all parts promote perspiration, stimulate appetite, and are used to treat ailments of the chest and digestion. Young leaves and shoots used to flavor wines and liqueurs, while the stout stems are candied as a cake decoration or cooked like rhubarb. Fresh or preserved roots have been added to snuff and used by Laplanders and North American Indians as tobacco.

Cultivation: sow fresh seeds outdoors in autumn for exposure to frost, or pre-chill in a refrigerator for a few weeks before sowing in spring. Transplant to a moist shady position as young as possible, before the roots become immovable.

Parts used: young leaves can be gathered any time during the growing season, the stems in the summer of the second year. Cut seedheads and ripen until seeds are dry enough to store. Roots are dug up just before flowering and dried slowly.

Related species: *A. atropurpurea*: a wild North American species used by Shakers as flavoring and medicine.

Anthriscus cerefolium (Umbelliferae)
❧ **Chervil**
salad chervil, garden beaked parsley

Description: decorative annual, sometimes grown as a biennial, 2 ft, with a tapering rootstock. A well-branched plant with sweet-scented and delicately cut pale foliage rather like parsley, and umbels of small white flowers in spring and summer, followed by large seedpods. Sometimes found wild as a garden escape, when it closely resembles young cow parsley (*A. sylvestris*). **Caution:** do not gather from the wild, as chervil may be confused with poisonous hemlock, fool's parsley and water dropwort.

Uses: leaves used in soups, salads and vinegars, and for garnishes. Medicinally the bruised plant is applied fresh or as poultices to wounds; an infusion aids digestion and encourages perspiration.

Cultivation: sow spring, summer or autumn *in situ* in rows or patches, in moisture-retentive soil in full sun or light shade. As plants often run to seed rapidly, sow little and often, or leave plants to self-seed. Sow in warmth for out-of-season supplies indoors.

Parts used: leaves gathered fresh as needed, and frozen or gently dried for storing. Roots sometimes dug and used in salad preparations.

Related species: Chaerophyllum bulbosum (bulbous chervil): a wild plant with tuberous roots; a close relative of *C. tenuilentum* (rough chervil).

Aquilegia vulgaris (Ranunculaceae)
❧ **Columbine**
granny's bonnets, European crowfoot

Description: tough-rooted herbaceous perennial with prettily cut leaves on wiry stems, 2 ft. Stout flowering stems in summer bear nodding spurred blooms in white, blue or pink. Found wild in meadows and waste places on chalky soils. Many garden forms with brilliant-colored flowers, often double or with extra-long spurs.

Uses: all parts have been used medicinally, but now usually grown only as a decorative plant for herb gardens. Roots, flowers and leaves have antiseptic properties, and roots were once used to treat ulcers. **Caution:** internal use is not recommended as aquilegias contain prussic acid, and all parts are poisonous, especially the seeds.

Cultivation: sow in rows in a nursery bed in late spring for transplanting in autumn; or sow early under glass, and plant out in summer after hardening off. Plant in moist soil in partially shady sites; dead-head garden forms promptly, as self-set seedlings tend to revert to wild form.

Arctium lappa (Compositae)
❧ **Greater Burdock**
beggar's buttons, lappa, cuckoo button, flapper-bags, bardana, clotburr, gipsy's rhizome

Description: short biennial with strong vertical roots up to 3 ft long, and a rosette of large coarse white-backed leaves like rhubarb. In summer thick hairy stems, 6 ft, bear reddish-purple tubular flowers, followed by seedheads (burrs) with hooked spines, lasting all winter. A handsome wild plant of waste places and roadsides.

Uses: a plant of widespread and varied virtues, burdock is cultivated in Japan as a vegetable (*gobo*); used everywhere as a folk remedy for skin problems, especially psoriasis and eczema; grown in China for its seeds, used for throat and chest ailments. A wild vegetable used by North American Indians. The chopped root may be cooked, and the stalks treated like angelica (these contain inulin, a mildly sweet substance useful for diabetics). Roots used as flavoring.

Cultivation: usually gathered from the wild, but seeds may be sown *in situ* in rich, loamy soil in the wild garden.

Parts used: roots of 1-year-old plants, split and dried slowly; young shoots and peeled stalks (before flowering) for salads or as a cooked vegetable; dried seeds for medicinal use.

Related species: A. minus (common, lesser or small burdock): a similar plant, but with more pointed leaves and smaller seedheads.

Armeria maritima
(Plumbaginaceae)
🐌 **Thrift**
sea pink

Description: evergreen perennial forming mounds of narrow grassy leaves, 4-8 in, on woody rootstock. In early summer produces short-stemmed white or rose flowers with a strong scent of honey. Grows wild in sandy soil beside the sea, but often planted in gardens, sometimes in improved forms.

Uses: an infusion of fresh or dried flowers was formerly used as an antiseptic and to treat nervous disorders, but now thought to cause allergic reactions such as dermatitis. A valuable formal edging plant for herb gardens and for planting in paths; very popular with butterflies.

Cultivation: sow autumn or spring indoors in trays and plant out when hardened off. Tufts may be rooted as cuttings in a shaded frame in summer. Plant in full sun or light shade.

Related species: A. arenaria (Jersey thrift): plant of similar habit but altogether larger, with stout stems bearing deep pink flowers.

Armoracia rusticana, syn.
Cochlearia armoracia (Cruciferae)
🐌 **Horseradish**

Description: coarse herbaceous perennial. Long-stalked oval leaves, up to 3 ft long; umbels of off-white flowers in mid- to late summer. Pungent roots, up to 2 ft long.

Uses: used medicinally as a digestive, antiseptic and stimulant, and to make poultices for rheumatism, chest complaints and circulation problems. Young leaves may be used for flavoring in salads, or cooked; roots are often made into a sauce. **Caution:** use medicinally with care, as the roots may cause internal inflammation, affect the thyroid gland or, used externally, produce blisters.

Cultivation: although often grown as a perennial for occasional use, plants are invasive and virtually ineradicable, every fragment of bought-in root reviving to grow again. Better cultivated as an annual crop by burying 6 in long upper portions of bought-in roots about 12 in apart in ridges of rich soil in early spring. Water well in

dry weather, and in late autumn dig out all the roots for storing in boxes of moist sand.

Parts used: young leaves gathered in spring; roots dug in autumn.

Arnica montana (Compositae)
🐌 **Arnica**
mountain arnica, mountain daisy, mountain tobacco, fall dandelion, leopard's bane

Description: pungent ornamental perennial with creeping rhizomes and prostrate rosettes of downy leaves. Hairy flower stems, 1-2 ft, bear bright yellow daisies in summer and autumn. Grows wild in hilly and highland districts, but also often grown as garden ornamental.

Uses: homeopathic treatment for epilepsy and blood pressure. A formerly popular Shaker salve; used in many countries to treat bruises and sprains, and also for throat infections, wounds and paralysis. Included in some French herbal smoking mixtures. **Caution:** poisonous and not for self-medication, as the plant may be toxic and cause skin irritations.

Cultivation: sow seeds in a cold frame in spring (germination may be slow) and plant out in autumn in sandy acid soils in full sun; divide mature roots in autumn or spring.

Parts used: whole top growth, especially flowers, either fresh or after drying slowly in shade; roots dug up in late spring or autumn and dried in artificial heat.

Artemisia (Compositae)

A large genus of aromatic shrubs and herbaceous perennials, some with finely cut ornamental foliage ranging in color from gray-green to bright silver. Most shrubby kinds are adapted to hot dry places in full sun, and, apart from their medicinal uses, provide valuable color and form in the herb garden. Only the commonest types are described here.

Artemisia abrotanum
Southernwood
lad's love, old man, Crusader herb

Description: graceful woody perennial shrub, up to 3 ft, with pungent feathery leaves, gray-green and downy. Inconspicuous yellow-green daisy-shaped flowers in late summer.

Uses: like all the artemisias, named after the Greek goddess Artemis, who had special care of women. Used medicinally as an infusion or tincture to regulate menstruation, but also as an antiseptic, insect repellent (in mothballs) and air freshener; used by medieval Crusaders to ward off plague. Has a reputation as a hair-wash and bitter stimulant, and even as an aphrodisiac. Stems yield a yellow dye.

Cultivation: prefers to be grown in sun, in well-drained soil. Propagate from soft cuttings in summer, or semi-ripe cuttings with a 'heel' in autumn. Cut back new growth of shrubs by half every spring, and disbud to prevent flowering. An ideal low hedge if trimmed in spring and again in summer.

Parts used: shoots and leaves, which may be dried slowly in the sun.

Artemisia dracunculus
French tarragon
estragon, serpentarian

Description: herbaceous perennial of shrubby growth, with slim woody branching stems 3 ft. Smooth, dark green pointed leaves, and woolly white or grey flowers in late summer. Spreads by creeping rootstocks, which may be invasive.

Uses: popular culinary herb for stimulating the appetite and flavoring sauces, preserves and cooked dishes. Historically used for toothache, and by the Romans to treat snakebite. Useful for catarrhal and digestive problems, while tarragon tea is used to cure insomnia. An ingredient of perfumes and liqueurs.

Cultivation: may only be propagated by dividing the roots in spring or autumn, or from soft cuttings taken in early summer. Grow in rich, well-drained soil and confine roots in the same way as for mint. Renew every three years or so, and mulch in winter to protect roots. Young roots may be potted up for winter supplies but benefit from a dormant period.

Parts used: growing tips gathered for fresh use; all top growth may be harvested at flowering time for drying slowly in gentle heat.

Related species: *A. dracunculoides* (Russian tarragon): a more robust, coarser plant that may be raised from seed, as well as by division and from cuttings. Tolerates a wider range of soil types, but markedly inferior in flavor. Similar uses, but does not dry successfully.

Artemisia vulgaris
Mugwort
felon herb, St John's herb, moxa

Description: herbaceous perennial with red-purple stems up to 6 ft. Long green ferny leaves with white undersides, and numerous reddish-brown flowers in late summer. Com-mon in built-up areas and roadsides.

Uses: one of the nine Saxon magic herbs, used to make a tea for gastritis and digestive ailments, and to treat menstrual disorders. Insect repellent, and ingredient for herbal tobaccos and Chinese treatments for rheumatism. Used in stuffings for fatty meats. Leaves have been used to make fumigant candle wicks, flowers to flavor beer before the advent of hops. ***Caution:*** may be harmful when taken internally in excessive doses.

Cultivation: may be grown from seeds sown *in situ* in spring and thinned to about 12 in apart, in sun and light shade. Allow plenty of room, as plants grow quickly to full height. Take cuttings in autumn, or divide roots in autumn or spring. Take care that plants do not become invasive.

Parts used: all parts of the plant, either fresh or dried slowly in the shade.

Related species: A. verlotiorum: an Asian wild species, used in Chinese medicine.

Asparagus officinalis (Liliaceae)
❧ **Asparagus**
sparrow grass, sperage

Description: herbaceous perennial, up to 6 ft. Young, scaly edible 'spears' in spring grow into tall branched stems bearing fine ferny green needles. Greenish-white flowers appear in summer, followed on female plants by red berries in autumn. Fern or 'bower' turns bright yellow as it dies. Found wild on coasts, and widespread in the Middle East; stems may be prostrate.

Uses: an ornamental plant and early summer vegetable. Medicinally used as a laxative, while a tea brewed from the mature fern has been used for rheumatic and urinary disorders, and by Shakers to treat dropsy.

Cultivation: seeds may be sown in rows in spring, the strongest seedlings thinned to 6 in apart; transplant 2 ft apart the following spring in beds or single rows in light rich well-drained soil (on heavy ground create raised beds of suitable soil). Alternatively plant bought 1- or 2-year-old crowns. Start cropping when plants are 3 years old, cutting the 6-8 in high spears just below ground level from spring until midsummer (in parts of Europe the spears are first blanched by earthing up plants). Use largest spears for eating, thinner ones ('sprue') medicinally. Cut down fern and top-dress beds every autumn with compost.

Parts used: young stems ('spears' or 'tips') and fern; roots sometimes dug up for medicinal purposes.

Atriplex hortensis (Chenopodiaceae)
❧ **Orach(e)**
(red) mountain spinach

Description: an erect leafy annual, up to 2-3 ft or sometimes taller still. Triangular fleshy leaves are dark green, or red in the attractive form *A. hortensis rubra* (red mountain spinach). Thread-like spikes of green or red flowers appear in summer. Common wild on sandy waste land, shingle beaches and salty sites.

Uses: traditional wild herb, often cultivated as a vegetable and garden ornamental; used as a spring tonic and stimulant, and in infusions to treat tiredness or exhaustion.

Cultivation: sow *in situ* in spring in sunny positions, either in rows or broadcast in small patches. Pinch out growing tips once and harvest shoots before plants flower, as they self-seed prolifically.

Parts used: larger leaves and whole young shoots.

Related species: *A. patula* (common orach, ironroot): mealy gray leaves and often trailing stems; common wild on warm beaches, used as a green vegetable.

A. prostrata (hastate orach): similar wild species with much larger leaves.

Borago officinalis (Boraginaceae)
❧ **Borage**
burage, bugloss, bee bread, bee plant

Description: stout herb, with hollow, bristly stems growing to 2-3 ft. Broad oval leaves, also stiffly hairy, and heavy bent clusters of blue star-shaped flowers (white form occasionally found), popular with bees, followed by oval seed capsules. A cultivated herb, sometimes occurring on waste ground.

Uses: a popular reviver included in some drinks. Young leaves add the flavor of cucumber to salads, older ones can be used as a vegetable, while in France and Italy the flowers are often cooked in batter as fritters. An infusion of leaves and seeds was a folk method of increasing the milk supply of nursing mothers, and to treat coughs, cold and depression. The roots are used to flavor wine, and the seeds are a source of gamma-linoleic acid, an essential fatty acid thought to reduce the risk of arteriosclerosis.

Cultivation: sow in early spring (outdoors or in pots) for flowers the same year, or in late summer outdoors to produce larger biennial plants that flower early the following summer. Grow in well drained soil in full sun. Plants self-seed freely to produce seedlings that usually overwinter safely.

Parts used: leaves and stems (latter said to have greater stimulating properties); flowers used fresh, candied, or dried in moderate heat and kept well sealed; seeds dried for medicinal use; roots dug after flowering.

Buxus sempervirens (Buxaceae)
🌿 **Common Box**
boxwood, box tree

Description: a slow-growing evergreen shrub, occasionally small tree, up to 16 ft. Crowded oval leathery leaves, shiny and dark green above, paler beneath. Small greenish-white flowers in mid-spring, male and female blooms in separate groups. Grows wild on chalky commons, but widely cultivated as a garden ornamental, especially as formal hedges since the dense growth tolerates frequent clipping.

Uses: leaves yield a red dye, and are used homeopathically to treat fevers and rheumatism and to promote sweating. One of the best shrubs for topiary and hedges, the compact 'Suffruticosa' being the form grown as dwarf hedging around formal flower and herb beds. **Caution:** the foliage is too toxic for amateur medicinal use.

Cultivation: plant autumn or spring in rich, light soil, preferably in full sun although light shade is tolerated. Keep well watered and feed annually in spring. For hedging choose young plants and space them about 4 in apart, as older ones have very large rootballs and need more space when planted; trim in spring and again at midsummer for formal appearance. Propagate from cuttings outdoors in early autumn, or by layering lower branches.

Parts used: leaves at any time; bark and timber from larger pruned branches.

Related species: B. macowanii (Cape box): very similar species used for the same purposes in South Africa.

Calendula officinalis (Compositae)
🌿 **(Pot) Marigold**
common marigold, marybud, marygold, English marigold

Description: perennial herb, usually grown as an annual or biennial, with sticky angular stems up to 2 ft. Long oval leaves, hairy and fleshy, larger at the base; solitary yellow-orange flowers from early summer. Many cultivated forms in a range of yellow, orange and brown, often double.

Uses: apart from being popular old-fashioned cottage garden plants, pot marigolds have a long history of medicinal use. A tea made from the flowers is used for internal spasms and gastric disorders, but the main reputation is as an antiseptic and anti-inflammatory healer of wounds; a common ingredient of many proprietary salves and ointments. Used by Shakers to treat gangrene. Petals can be used as a hair rinse, a coloring agent for butter and cheese, and a substitute for the color of saffron. Also used in cooking and as a garnish.

Cultivation: sow *in situ* in full sun or light shade, in spring for late flowering, or (better) in autumn to overwinter and make bushy plants that flower over a long season the following year. Dead-head regularly to prolong flowering. Although plants thrive best on heavier ground, they tend to self-seed most on light soils.

Parts used: petals fresh or dried in the shade; young fresh leaves in salads; whole flowers boiled as a dye.

Campanula rapunculus (Campanulaceae)
🌿 **Rampion**
rampion bellflower

Description: herbaceous biennial with thick fleshy turnip-like taproot, and slim straight angular stems to 3 ft with milky sap. Slim, toothed leaves, oval near plant base; overwinters as a low rosette, producing in the second year pale blue or white star-shaped flowers in midsummer. A wild plant of meadows, fields and hedgerows.

Uses: an ornamental wild flower, whose leaves are used in winter salads. Popular enough in the sixteenth and seventeenth centuries to be cultivated as a root vegetable (but note that 'German rampion' is the root of evening primrose).

Cultivation: for leaves, sow in spring for autumn use, and in early summer for winter crops. For roots, sow in rich soil in a shady position in the kitchen garden, in rows 8 in apart and thin seedlings to the same distance; sow in spring, but if plants flower early in a hot season, sow again in summer.

Parts used: leaves gathered any time before flowering; roots dug from autumn onwards – may be stored in sand in a cool place.

Centaurium erythraea, syn.
Erythraea centaurium
(Gentianaceae)

(Common) Centaury

bitterherb, centaury gentian, feverwort

Description: a delicate annual growing to 12 in, often less. From a rosette of elliptical gray-green pointed leaves, several stems produce branching umbels of tubular flowers in late summer, pink with yellow centers, arranged in clusters and closing when rain is imminent. Found wild in damp meadows and grassy woodlands.

Uses: an ancient Greek and Celtic medicinal herb, used to make a poultice for skin disorders; taken as a bitter tonic by North American Indians. A tea made from the whole plant treats digestive disorders including heartburn, while homeopathic preparation is prescribed for the liver and gall bladder. One of the aromatic ingredients of vermouth.

Cultivation: although growing wild in damp places, it will adapt to most garden soils, thriving and self-seeding in sun or semi-shade in rock gardens and near the sea. Sow in autumn or spring where plants are to grow, and barely cover the seeds.

Parts used: whole plant gathered at flowering time and dried quickly in shade outdoors or in a warm room.

Related species: C. littorale (seaside centaury): smaller, with narrower leaves, flower paler but larger. A plant found on sand dunes, with similar uses.

Sabatia stellaris (American centaury): a biennial of marshes and wet localities, with similar uses.

Centaurea nigra

Knapweed

lesser knapweed, black knapweed

Description: tough perennial with sturdy ridged stems and dark green hairy leaves. Grows up to 3 ft. Tubular purple flowers in summer. Grows wild on wasteland, roadsides and as a cliff plant.

Uses: a medieval wound salve; used to soothe sore throats and bleeding gums. Also acts as a diuretic.

Cultivation: grows easily in any soil; needs no particular attention. Self-seeds freely. May need containment.

Chamaemelum nobile, syn.
Anthemis nobilis (Compositae)

Lawn Chamomile

Roman chamomile, double chamomile, common chamomile, perennial chamomile

Description: a vigorous hairy creeping perennial, up to 18 in, with ferny leaves and apple-scented white and yellow flowers in summer; non-flowering forms available for creating lawns. Grows wild in stony ground.

Uses: popular since early Egyptian times, a traditional strewing herb, and often used by Arabs in the form of the essential oil. Ingredient of a famous herb tea for settling nervous disorders, stimulating the appetite and cleansing the blood. Made into herb beers and tisanes, hair rinses and eye lotions, as well as being used in the preparation of cosmetics and perfumes. Essential oil is said to revive cut flowers. Plants often grown as herbal lawns and on ornamental seats.

lawn chamomile

(Continued)

*(**Lawn Chamomile** continued)*

Cultivation: sow seeds in spring outdoors or under cover, but do not cover as the seeds need light for germination. Established plants may be divided in spring, the only way to propagate named forms. Plant in fertile, well-drained light soil, 18 in apart for specimen plants and 6 in for lawns, and be sure to water well in dry weather.

Parts used: whole plant for distillation; flowers for essential oil and teas, collected as petals begin to reflex in the sun; dried rapidly in shade.

double chamomile

Related species: *A. arvensis* (corn chamomile), *A. cotula* (stinking chamomile), *Tripleurospermum inodorum* (scentless mayweed): all similar-looking wild flowers with wholly or partly downy leaves, but without the characteristic pleasant subtle apple fragrance.

True wild chamomile is *Matricaria recutita*, q.v.

Chelidonium majus
(Papaveraceae)
Greater Celandine
swallow-wort, tetterwort

Description: herbaceous perennial with brittle fleshy branching stems up to 3 ft, with soft, finely hairy leaves, yellowish above and blue-green beneath, divided into toothed leaflets. Numerous small yellow flowers appear in summer (double form also available), followed by erect green seed capsules. All parts contain an acrid bright orange sap that may be irritating to the skin.

Uses: once widely grown as a decorative cottage garden herb, but now regarded as a weed of waste and cultivated ground, and walls. Antispasmodic and mildly sedative, traditionally valued for its sap as a treatment for warts and source of an orange dye. Flowers are beneficial for thyroid conditions, while the roots have been used to treat liver and gall bladder disorders. **Caution:** in large doses may be poisonous, and an internal and external irritant.

Cultivation: sow seeds in autumn or divide roots in spring, and plant in dry chalky soils in sun or light shade. Plants normally seed freely but are rarely a nuisance.

Parts used: top growth at flowering time, fresh or dried slowly in darkness; sap at any time from top growth or dormant roots; roots dug in autumn.

Chenopodium bonus-henricus
(Chenopodiaceae)
Good King Henry
all-good, mercury, poor man's asparagus

Description: herbaceous perennial with smooth, slightly fluted stems up to 2 ft 6 in, and thick fleshy triangular leaves, gray and mealy at first. Small yellow-green flowers in clusters appear at midsummer. Found wild on light, rich soils, but often cultivated.

Uses: cultivated as an early green spinach-like crop, the first shoots sometimes blanched by earthing up for use like asparagus.

Cultivation: sow in spring *in situ* or in a seedbed, and thin or plant at 18 in distances in light, fertile soil. Plants seed freely, so dead-head to prevent invasiveness.

Parts used: young leaves and shoots.

Related species: *C. album* (fat hen, common pigweed, common lambs-quarter, white goosefoot): red-stemmed salad ingredient, tonic herb for livestock and source of a red dye; seeds once used for flour.

C. ambrosioides anthelmiticum (American wormseed), Mexican tea): annual wild plant, source of chenopodium oil widely used for the treatment of internal worms. **Caution:** large doses may be poisonous.

C. quinoa (quinoa): Peruvian annual, widely cultivated in South America.

C. botrys (ambrosia), *C. leptophyllum*, *C. nuttaliae*: other sources of fatty and nutritious seeds.

Coriandrum sativum
(Umbelliferae)
🐌 **Coriander**
cilantro

Description: rigid, strong-smelling annual with pronounced taproot, and slender stems up to 2 ft. Ferny pinnate leaves, rounded and parsley-like at base, and umbels of small white or pink flowers in midsummer, followed by round red-brown seed capsules, aromatic when ripe. Many named forms selected for leaf or seed production; small-seeded varieties are usually grown in temperate regions, large-seeded kinds in warmer climates. Grows wild in bare places, usually as an escape from cultivation.

Uses: one of the oldest recorded spices, mentioned in ancient Sanskrit texts and in Exodus (coriander is one of the bitter Passover herbs). The leaves and shoots are added to salads, soups and stews, especially in India, South America and China (the leaf is sometimes known as 'Chinese parsley'). The seeds are a stimulant and digestive, often ground and included in curries and regional meat dishes. They are used as a flavoring for bread, and yield an essential oil for soaps and perfumes. They are sometimes added to pot-pourri, and to other herbs to disguise their unpalatability. The root supplies a stronger flavoring, and is often cooked as a vegetable in South-East Asia.

Cultivation: sow *in situ* in autumn or spring, and thin to 6 in apart. Grows fast in full sun, in well-drained soil with a little lime. Protect the brittle stems from wind. Plants usually self-seed freely. Several sowings are advisable for good leaf production.

Parts used: young leaves and shoots at any time; mature seeds dried, roasted and pulverized before use; roots dug after flowering.

Cymbopogon citratus (Gramineae)
🐌 **Lemon Grass**
oil grass, takrai, sereh

Description: coarse tufted tender perennial grass, lemon-scented, with strong roots and spear-shaped, brownish-green leaves up to 3 ft, growing from a tough, fibrous bulbous base.

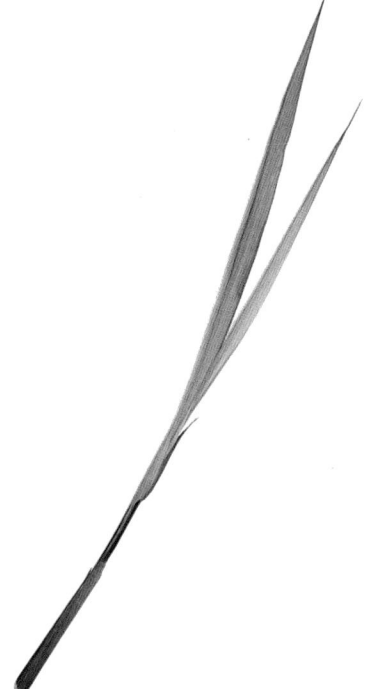

Uses: leaf buds and chopped stems are added to oriental dishes, and made into a tea for liver complaints. The plant yields lemon-grass oil, rich in vitamin A, which is used as a tonic and stimulant, antiseptic, and oily skin cleanser, as an ingredient of cosmetics, and as an aromatherapy oil.

Cultivation: divide clumps and plant offsets with their bottom 1 in buried in rich soil in a warm, sunny site sheltered from cold winds.

Parts used: leaf buds; stems fresh and finely chopped, or dried and ground.

Related species: *C. flexuosus* (Indian lemon grass): an alternative source of lemon-grass oil and an antiseptic.

C. martinii (ginger grass): a source of ginger-grass oil and palma-rosa oil.

C. nardus (citronella grass): yields Ceylon citronella oil for perfumery.

Cynara cardunculus
🐌 **Cardoon**

Description: a close relative of the thistle and globe artichoke, this short-lived perennial grows up to 6 ft. Impressive silvery leaves, ridged stems, often grown as an ornamental garden plant. Gray-blue thistle-like flowers appear in late summer.

Uses: an ornamental garden favorite, also an edible vegetable crop with a delicate flavor. Especially popular in Mediterranean countries. Best eaten in winter and spring.

Cultivation: from seed in almost any soil. To increase yield, cut down to ground level in early summer, feed and water copiously. New growth will be produced until well into autumn.

Parts used: stems, blanched, braised or fried; also added to sauces.

Cynoglossum officinale
(Boraginaceae)
🐚 **Hound's Tongue**
gipsy flower, rats-and-mice

Description: hairy gray-green herbaceous biennial, smelling of mice, with stems up to 3 ft. Leaves roughly hairy, large and oval or tongue-shaped near base of plant, upper ones much narrower. Clusters of hooded flowers, dull maroon or occasionally white, appear in midsummer, followed by hard, flat fruits covered with short-hooked spines. A wild plant of dry, grassy areas, especially near woods.

Uses: infusion from shaved root or crushed leaves used to bathe cuts, bruises, burns and eczema, and to treat coughs and bronchitis; leaves produce a potent poultice for external relief. A nectar-rich plant for bees and butterflies. **Caution:** self-medication is not recommended, as internal use can be dangerous, and external applications may cause dermatitis.

Cultivation: usually gathered from the wild, but seeds may be sown in late summer *in situ*: these need frost to stimulate germination and will not appear before the following spring. Grow in light, well-drained soils in full sun. Plants succeed in seaside gardens, and self-seed freely.

Parts used: flowers and leaves, fresh or dried in shade or a warm room; root fresh or dried.

Related species: C. germanicum (green hound's tongue): a similar plant, with leaves shiny and hairless, and lacking the distinctive odor of *C. officinale.*

Dianthus caryophyllus
(Caryophyllaceae)
🐚 **(Clove) Pink**
(clove) gillyflower, carnation, sops-in-wine, divine flower

Description: an evergreen perennial with gray-green branched stems 2-3 ft divided into sections by hard knuckles or nodes, from which long, thick gray-green waxy leaves, stiff and smooth-edged, arise in pairs often joined at their base. Showy, very fragrant flowers, rose-pink or white, appear in summer and early autumn. Found wild on walls and in chalky places in warm climates; cultivated in numerous forms and colors, especially as perpetual-flowering and border carnations.

Uses: an outstanding ornamental plant, whose fresh flowers are used in tonics, and to flavor drinks and syrups; dried petals are often added to pot-pourri.

Cultivation: easily grown on light, well-drained chalky soil in full sun. May be raised from seed sown under glass in spring, the seedlings potted on or transplanted outdoors to a nursery bed for planting in autumn. Propagate named forms from pipings in summer, or cuttings with a heel in early autumn.

Parts used: flowers, fresh or dried. Before culinary use remove the bitter petal base.

Related species: D. plumarius (cottage pink, grass pink): smaller plant with slender rough-edged leaves, and fringed flowers in white, pink or purple; one of the parents of the garden pink.

Dryopteris filix-mas
🐚 **Male Fern**

Description: a fern with large fronds which grow up to 4 ft. Veins on the underside of fronds are covered with sporangia. Grows in damp woodlands and in hilly and mountainous areas.

Uses: once used to expel tapeworms, and formerly believed to soothe wounds, cure rickets and ease rheumatism. **Caution:** recent research suggests many species of fern are carcinogenic; male fern should be avoided; it should never be taken internally, especially not by those suffering from cardiac problems or by pregnant women.

Cultivation: grows freely in damp areas and on hedge banks. Should be avoided in the herb garden because of possible health risks.

Echium vulgare (Boraginaceae)

⚘ **Viper's Bugloss**
blue weed, blue devil

Description: herbaceous biennial with an exceptionally long drought-resistant taproot and coarse, hairy stems up to 3 ft. Grayish freckled leaves, long and narrow with rounded tips near the base of the plant, shorter on the flowering stem. Plants flower at midsummer, the dense panicles of pink buds opening into bright blue flowers with long, conspicuous stamens. A wild plant of dry, stony or grassy places, often near the sea; cultivated blue or white forms grown in gardens.

Uses: an outstanding ornamental plant, originally used to treat snakebite (both the seeds and stem markings resemble the features of snakes), the whole plant being crushed and applied to the bite. Flowers are mildly tonic and antiseptic, and may be added to drinks or candied. Leaves may be cooked like spinach.

Cultivation: sow in late summer in any soil where plants are to flower, and thin seedlings to 18 in apart; transplant others to new sites while still young and their taproots undeveloped. Plants self-seed freely where happy.

Parts used: fresh young leaves and shoots before flowering; flowers when fully open.

Related species: *E. lycopsis* (purple viper's bugloss): more softly hairy, with larger red-purple flowers and fewer stamens. Similar uses.

Eruca vesicaria spp. *sativa* (Cruciferae)

⚘ **(Garden or Sweet) Rocket**
rocket-salad, rocket-gentle, rocquette

Description: fast-growing annual, with a rosette of smooth, dark green leaves, indented like a dandelion. Branched, leafy main stems, hairy and reddish, growing to 2 ft, producing sparse simple flowers of loose, floppy creamy-yellow petals with purple veins, followed by fat, crisp seedpods.

Uses: salad herb with pungent flavor, especially popular in Mediterranean countries. A tonic, mild stimulant and cough remedy. Crisp seedpods are edible, seeds used to treat bruises and supply mustard oils.

Cultivation: for succulent leaves grow in rich, moist soil in full sun or light shade; on hot, dry soils plants run to seed quickly and produce tough, bitter leaves. Sow in spring and again at midsummer (all year round in warm districts), and keep well watered. Plants usually self-seed.

Parts used: leaves gathered in succession as soon as plants are large enough; seedpods while young and juicy; seeds from ripe seedpods.

Eupatorium perfoliatum (Compositae)

⚘ **Boneset**
thoroughwort, agueweed

Description: perennial herbaceous herb, with branching rough stem up to 5 ft. Long narrow pointed leaves, dark green and shiny above, and white and downy beneath. Dense heads of small white, occasionally blue, flowers, followed by feathery seedheads.

Uses: a popular tonic and stimulant, best known as a hot infusion for treating coughs and colds, or as an ointment or syrup for muscular aches.

Cultivation: sow on the surface of seed trays in autumn or spring in a cold frame; divide mature plants in spring or autumn, and grow in damp or marshy soil in sun or light shade.

Parts used: whole plant as flowers open, fresh or dried quickly in warmth.

Related species: *E. ayapana*: Brazilian species, producing a stimulant and digestive tea.

E. cannabinum (hemp agrimony, water hemp): contains eupatorin, used to treat dropsy; flowering herb or root also used as a tonic and laxative.

E. purpureum (joe-pye weed, gravel-root, queen of the meadow): white- and purple-flowered plant up to 10 ft; North American Indian red dye plant; roots and seedheads used to treat rheumatism, backache and urinary disorders.

Filipendula ulmaria, syn. *Spiraea ulmaria* (Rosaceae)

🌿 **Meadowsweet**

queen of the meadows, meadsweet, meadwort

Description: herbaceous perennial with a pink aromatic creeping rootstock. Reddish stems, up to 4 ft, bear pinnate leaves. Dense panicles of fragrant, creamy-white flowers in late summer.

Uses: an early source of salicylic acid. Tea from the flowers reduces fever, and is used to treat stomach acidity, influenza and rheumatism. Flower buds produce oil for perfume, and the dried flowers are added to home-made wines. Leaves flavor drinks, especially beer and mead. Dyes made from the roots (black) and flowers (yellow).

Cultivation: sow in spring or autumn *in situ* or in trays of compost under glass, or divide roots in spring. Plant in moist, rich soil in sun or light shade.

Parts used: flowers fresh or dried gently in warmth; roots dried for homeopathic use; leaves for flavoring.

Related species: *F. vulgaris* (dropwort): smaller plant, up to 2 ft, with less dense flowerheads. Roots sometimes used as a vegetable.

F. rubra, syn. *F. magnifica* (queen of the prairie): similar North American species with pink flowers.

Foeniculum vulgare (Umbelliferae)

🌿 **Fennel**

spigel

Description: grayish-green, strong-smelling herbaceous perennial, with slim stems up to 6 ft, bearing soft lacy, dark green leaves with thread-like lobes and swollen bases. Creeping rootstock gradually extends plant into a sparse clump. Small mustard-yellow flowers appear in summer, followed by small egg-shaped seedpods. Grows wild in waste places and damp sites; may become an invasive weed, as in Australia and New Zealand.

Uses: one of nine Anglo-Saxon sacred herbs; much used by ancient Greeks and throughout the Middle Ages. Roots once boiled as a vegetable, and used as an expectorant in cough mixtures. Dried stalks are an essential ingredient of Provençal cuisine. Soft growing tips are widely used to flavor and garnish fish dishes, soups and baked foods, and may be made into fennel tea to treat indigestion and colic. A popular flavoring for liqueurs and a scent for soaps and cosmetics. Oil produced from seeds is antibacterial. In warmer regions foliage attracts swallowtail butterflies. **Caution:** avoid large doses.

Cultivation: for lavish growth light, moist soils are best. Divide roots in spring and plant in a warm sunny place, or sow seeds in spring or summer, either in pots or *in situ* 20 in apart. Roots become long and tough, so transplant while still young. Water well in dry weather. Fennel self-seeds freely, so dead-head if seeds not needed. Plants become congested and exhausted after 3-4 years, and are then best replaced. Do not grow near dill, as these two species cross-fertilize readily to produce useless hybrids.

Parts used: growing tips, fresh or dried in early summer (leaves and stems may be cropped several times before flowering); seeds, from seedheads cut in autumn before fully mature and dried in warmth; roots dug in autumn and dried slowly.

Related species: *F. vulgare* 'Dulce' (Florence fennel, finocchio, sweet fennel): annual cropped from the wild for its essential oil, and cultivated as a vegetable for its juicy, swollen stem base.

F. vulgare 'Piperitum' (carosella, cartucci): local Italian vegetable with blanched young stems.

Ferula foetida (asafoetida): perennial herb used as an Indian condiment and in sauces; medicinal resin extracted from the root.

Ferula galbaniflua (galbanum): Middle Eastern species, the stem and roots of which yield an aromatic gum used for incense.

Fragaria vesca (Rosaceae)

🐌 (Wild) Strawberry

wood strawberry

Description: deciduous herbaceous perennial, spreading by runners or stolons. Single white flowers on stems in summer, followed by red or white berries with numerous yellow seeds on the outside. Grows wild in woods and grassy places on dry soil.

Uses: mildly laxative fruits are a nerve tonic, rich in iron. Leaves can be made into a popular tea that is a diuretic and astringent; fresh leaves sometimes added to salads. **Caution:** excessive consumption sometimes leads to allergic reactions.

Cultivation: plant young runners in spring or autumn, or sow seeds under glass in spring (sow on the surface and keep moist – germination may be slow and erratic). Plant in sun or light shade, in any soil except clay.

Parts used: fruit when fully colored; leaves at any time; roots dug in winter.

Related species: *F. moschata* (hautbois strawberry, musk strawberry): wild species with larger flowers.

F. virginiana (wild strawberry): red-fruited wild species, an important North American Indian legendary and medicinal plant, and one parent of most large-fruited forms.

Galium odoratum, syn. *Asperula odorata* (Rubiaceae)

🐌 (Sweet) Woodruff

kiss-me-quick, master of the woods (Waldmeister)

Description: herbaceous perennial, often evergreen. Branched stems up to 12 in bear neat whorls of dark green leaves. Clusters of star-shaped flowers on long stalks appear in early summer.

Uses: flavors wines and other drinks, and scents linen, pot-pourri and perfumes. Medicinally used to poultice wounds and scabies, and to stimulate milk flow of nursing mothers. **Caution:** excessive use may produce dizziness and respiratory allergies.

Cultivation: divide roots at any time, or sow ripe seeds in late summer *in situ.* Grow in rich, alkaline soil in shade, and harvest from second year onwards.

Parts used: green plant cut at or just before flowering time, and dried slowly.

Related species: *G. verum* (lady's bed-straw): taller and with thinner leaves; sweet-scented yellow flowers used to curdle milk and color cheese; stems yield a red dye.

Asperula tinctoria (dyer's woodruff): white-flowered species, giving a yellow-orange dye.

Gaultheria procumbens (Ericaceae)

🐌 Wintergreen

partridge berry, tea berry, chequerberry

Description: evergreen perennial shrub with prostrate creeping stems from which erect branches grow to 6 in high. Top of each branch bears a few leathery, serrated oval leaves, shiny and paler beneath. Drooping white or pink flowers appear in midsummer, followed by pea-sized scarlet berries. A wild plant growing in woodlands on acid soils.

Uses: leaves made into aromatic infusion for use as a gargle. Leaves are pain-reducing, and when dried can be made into a tea. Oil distilled from the leaves rubbed in externally to treat muscular aches and pains, and also used to flavor dental preparations.

Cultivation: excellent ground-cover plant for moist, acid soils and rock gardens. Plant in autumn or spring in peaty soils in full sun or light shade. Propagate by seeds sown in a seedbed outdoors in autumn, or from rooted prostrate stems in spring.

Parts used: leaves fresh or dried in the sun, distilled for oil of wintergreen.

Related species: *G. antipoda:* New Zealand species, either prostrate or a medium-sized shrub, with edible red berries.

G. shallon (shallon, salal): vigorous, shrubby North American species, with purple berries.

Genista tinctoria (Leguminosae)

❧ **Dyer's Greenweed**

dyer's broom

Description: dwarf deciduous broom-like shrub, sometimes prostrate or erect to 3 ft. Bright green branches and narrow pointed glossy leaves; long, leafy racemes of bright yellow pea-type flowers in summer. A wild plant of dry grassy places and heaths; numerous cultivated forms, including one with double flowers.

Uses: a decorative ground-cover plant to grow with heathers. Infusion made from young flowering shoots is diuretic and laxative, and used to treat dropsy and skin disorders. Young flower buds may be pickled like capers. Flowers yield a yellow dye, rich green if mixed with woad.

Cultivation: poor soil in an open, sunny position with good drainage is ideal. Plant autumn or spring, or sow seeds outdoors in autumn after rubbing them between sheets of sandpaper; named varieties may be grafted on to laburnum rootstocks in spring. Prune soft growth after flowering.

Parts used: flower buds; flowers for dye; young flowering shoots fresh or dried in shade.

Geranium maculatum (Geraniaceae)

❧ **American Cranesbill**

spotted cranesbill, alum root, crowfoot

American cranesbill

Description: hairy herbaceous perennial with stout rhizomatous root and stems up to 2 ft. Leaves elegant and downy, divided with scalloped edges and blotched with white as they age. Small pink-purple, occasionally white, flowers appear in late spring, followed by fruits with long barbs like the bill of a crane. A wild plant of hedgerows and woodlands.

Uses: a popular North American Indian herb; root is astringent, used in infusions or as a powder to treat diarrhoea, dysentery and bleeding, and ulcers, both internal and external.

Cultivation: divide mature plants in early spring, or sow in autumn or spring where plants are to grow after rubbing seeds between sheets of sandpaper. Grow in full sun or light shade in moist, leafy soil. Plants self-seed profusely and soon develop into thick clumps.

Parts used: roots gathered in autumn or winter, dried and powdered.

herb robert

Related species: G. robertianum (herb robert, stinking cranesbill): annual with pink or white flowers; whole plant (including roots) is a powerful wound herb, used to stop bleeding and heal oral inflammations.

Phlomis fruticosa (Labiatae)
❧ Jerusalem Sage

Description: aromatic evergreen shrub with stout branching stems up to 10 ft. Silvery-green, wedge-shaped leaves are wrinkled and densely covered with yellow woolly hairs. Clear or rusty yellow tubular flowers appear in whorls in late summer. Grows wild in arid Mediterranean and Asian regions, and commonly grown as a shrub in herb and mixed borders.

Uses: mainly a handsome ornamental shrub; leaves sometimes made into an aromatic sage-flavored tea, especially in Greece and neighbouring Mediterranean countries.

Cultivation: sow seeds in spring, take cuttings in summer or divide in spring or autumn. Grow in dryish, well-drained soil in full sun.

Parts used: leaves, fresh or dried in the sun.

Plantago major (Plantaginaceae)
❧ Greater Plantain
broadleaf plantain, rat's tail plantain, waybread, white man's footprint

Description: tough-rooted perennial with coarse basal rosette of long-stalked, elliptical leaves, pointed and deeply veined. Tall, dense cylindrical spikes of tiny greenish-yellow flowers appear in summer, up to 18 in, followed by a spike of seeds enclosed in sticky gelatinous pods. Found wild in cultivated land, waste ground, lawns and footpaths, where the spread of its sticky seeds is helped by passers-by. A local field crop in France, and also cultivated in gardens in improved forms.

Uses: an old herb, one of the nine sacred Saxon species and recovered from remains of Iron Age Tollund Man. The crushed leaves are cooling and pain-relieving, used in poultices and ointments for wounds and abrasions; an infusion of leaves or boiled roots is a useful gargle and eyewash; fresh leaves may be taken for both constipation and diarrhoea, according to the dosage. Very young leaves may be cooked like spinach; seeds are popular in Chinese and Malaysian drinks, and complete seedheads are fed to caged birds.

Cultivation: wild variety rarely grown deliberately, but seeds may be sown *in situ*, barely covered, in moist, fertile light soil or loam, in spring or autumn. Plants self-seed freely.

Parts used: leaves, fresh or dried quickly in sun or shade; roots, dug in winter and boiled; seed spikes, gathered in bags when they turn brown, and rubbed to free the seeds.

Related species: *P. coronopus* (crowfoot plantain, buckshorn plantain): biennial with dandelion-like leaves, used in salads while very young.

P. lanceolata (ribwort plantain): perennial with long, narrow leaves and short dense ribbed stem of yellow-brown flowers, used as cough remedy and wound healer.

P. media (hoary plantain): decorative perennial with scented, pink and white fluffy flowers, a great favourite with bees.

P. ovata (ispaghula): annual with medicinal seeds, producing a laxative and emollient oil.

P. psyllium (fleaseed), *P. indica* (branched plantain): annuals with branching globular heads of greenish flowers; known in Latin America as *llanten*, used in same way as ispaghula.

Portulaca oleracea (Portulacaceae)
(Wild) Purslane
pigweed

Description: warm-climate annual, with fleshy pinkish stems, prostrate and branching to 12 in, bearing fleshy spatulate leaves, green or red-tinged. Small yellow flowers appear in the leaf axils in late summer, followed by seed capsules with opening lids and filled with numerous tiny black seeds. Grows wild in dry soils in vineyards and on hillsides in warm regions, a common weed in Australia, New Zealand and the United States; cultivated as an edible crop in the form var. *sativa* (kitchen-garden purslane), a larger erect plant with fleshy green or gold leaves.

Uses: ancient vegetable crop in India and Iran, still used as a salad herb and cooked vegetable. Infusion of the green plant is cooling and soothing, taken for fevers, headaches and chest complaints, and applied to skin rashes and abrasions. Seeds are an Australian Aboriginal wild condiment.

Cultivation: sow mid-spring in light, well-drained soil; water and feed regularly. Sow again for succession at monthly intervals until late summer.

Parts used: fresh leaves and stems, preferably before flowering, cut just above ground level.

Poterium sanguisorba, syn. *Sanguisorba minor* (Rosaceae)
Salad Burnet

Description: clump-forming perennial with strong woody rootstock, and red, furrowed stems branching to 2 ft. Gray-green pinnate leaves with rounded leaflets, each deeply indented, and small, bright red-brown petalless flowers in dense globular heads in early summer. Found wild in fields, woods and waste ground on dry chalk.

Uses: young leaves eaten as salad herb with cucumber-like flavor, and added to soups, sauces and cheeses. Leaves are digestive, and in infusions used to treat diarrhoea and haemorrhages. Decoction of root applied to cuts and burns; roots also produce a black dye and are used in tanning leather.

Cultivation: sow in spring in trays under glass, or divide roots in spring and plant in fertile soil in sun or light shade. Remove flowers to extend useful season for leaves. Plants self-seed very easily.

Parts used: young leaves before flowering; whole green plant, fresh or dried; roots dug in spring and dried.

Related species: *P. officinale*, syn. *Sanguisorba officinalis* (great burnet, bloodwort): taller herb with deep red, rectangular flowerheads; similar uses.

Prunella vulgaris (Labiatae)
Selfheal
heal-all, woundwort, carpenter's herb

Description: downy perennial with creeping rhizome and square stems to 12 in. Long narrow oval leaves, bright green, pointed and toothed; flowers purple, pink or white in dense whorls in midsummer. Grows wild in moist meadows and pastures; many cultivated forms with larger flowers grown in gardens.

Uses: used in Middle Ages according to the 'Doctrine of Signatures' to treat throat conditions and internal bleeding, and regarded as a panacea by North American Indians and Chinese physicians, the latter using the seeds for nervous complaints. Flowering plant may be eaten in salads and cooked vegetable dishes, used to prepare a styptic for wounds, and made into gargles or mouthwashes for mouth ulcers and sore throats.

Cultivation: take cuttings or divide plants in spring, and plant out 8 in apart as ground cover in moist shade or full sun. In fertile soils plants are much larger than normal and may be invasive; growing in turf helps restrain unnatural growth.

Parts used: green flowering plant, fresh or dried in shade.

Pulmonaria officinalis
(Boraginaceae)

🌿 **Lungwort**

maple lungwort, spotted dog,
Jerusalem cowslip

Description: downy perennial with
creeping rootstock; stems hairy and
unbranched, up to 12 in. Rough
leaves in a rosette over winter, broadly
oval and pointed, green with gray
spots, stem leaves narrower. Flowers
bell-shaped in small, leafy sprays, pink
at first and later becoming blue, or
white or purple, in early spring. Grows
wild in woods and hedgerows on
chalk; often cultivated as ground
cover in shade.

Uses: ancient cure for lung disorders
according to 'Doctrine of Signatures'.
Young leaves used as spring pot herb
in soups, stews and salads; flowering
plant made into a tea for gastro-
intestinal and pulmonary ailments;
homeopathically used for bronchitis
and colds. Powdered roots and lower
leaves are wound-healing.

Cultivation: divide in autumn or after
flowering, and plant in light soils, not
too dry, in shade or semi-shade. Lift,
divide and replant every 4-5 years.

Parts used: young fresh leaves gathered; green flowering plant, fresh or
dried; roots dug in winter, cut, dried
and powdered.

Related species: *P. saccharata*
(Bethlehem sage): larger plant,
with leaves heavily marked with silver, flowers appear as lilac, white or
blue; grown as a foliage plant; similar uses to *P. officinalis.*

Reseda luteola (Resedaceae)

🌿 **Weld**

dyer's rocket

Description: coarse unbranched biennial with an overwintering rosette of
long, narrow wavy-edged leaves. In
summer stout leafy stem, 5 ft, termi-
nates in long, slim spike of small
bright yellow or yellow-green flowers.
Found growing wild in dry disturbed
soils in chalky areas.

Uses: traditional dye plant, once widely cultivated or gathered from the wild
for brilliant yellow or reddish-yellow
color extracted from leaves, flowers
and stems.

Cultivation: sow seeds where plants are
to flower, in late summer in well-
drained, fertile soil with a little lime.
Seedlings appear in spring and should
be thinned to 18 in apart.

Parts used: whole green plant gathered
at flowering time.

Related species: *R. lutea* (wild
mignonette): similar to weld, but
shorter with divided, wrinkled
leaves; popular and decorative bee
and butterfly plant.

R. odorata (common mignonette):
perennial normally grown as an
annual, both outdoors and in pots,
for its intensely fragrant tiny yellow
and white flowers, from which oil is
extracted for perfume; a soothing
herb for calming nerves, healing
wounds, and treating asthma and
hayfever; once used to stuff pillows
as a remedy for insomnia.

Rosmarinus officinalis (Labiatae)

🌿 **Rosemary**

Description: dense, woody evergreen
perennial, up to 10 ft. Bushy stems
with cracked gray bark and downy
young shoots are covered with narrow
aromatic, hard leaves, dark and shiny
above, grayish beneath. Short racemes
of small blue flowers appear in early
summer. Grows wild on dry, rocky
slopes and cliffs in warm regions, and
widely cultivated both commercially
and in gardens in numerous forms.

Uses: ancient strewing herb and
Romany charm, hung up to ward off
evil; popular culinary flavoring added
to meat dishes, baked foods and
Mediterranean recipes. Leaves medicinally valuable and for treating depression, migraine, and disorders of the
liver and digestion. Leaves also made
into ointment for neuralgia, rheumatism, eczema and minor wounds, and
used in hair rinsesand mouthwashes.
Caution: excessive quantities or frequent use may cause poisoning.

Cultivation: sow seeds in trays in
spring, take cuttings in summer in a
cold frame, or layer plants in autumn.
Plant in well-drained, alkaline soil,
in a sunny position sheltered from
winds. Some forms are slightly tender
and may need protection in winter.

Parts used: leaves gathered at flowering time, used fresh or dried in shade.

109 🌿

Rubia tinctorum (Rubiaceae)
🐚 **Dyer's Madder**
dyer's cleavers

Description: herbaceous perennial with long fleshy complex yellow rootstock and red fibrous roots, and stiff square, prickly climbing stems up to 3 ft, with whorls of pale green bristly leaves, long and pointed. Clusters of small greenish-yellow flowers appear in midsummer, followed by blue-black berries. Grows wild in hedges and thickets on chalk, often as an escape from former wide cultivation.

Uses: infusions of leaves and stems treat constipation, and liver and bladder disorders; powdered root is wound-healing, often used for skin ulcers. Homeopathically used to treat anaemia and ailments of the spleen. Most popular use of the roots is as a variable red to purple dye.

Cultivation: sow seeds or divide plants in spring or autumn, and plant in deep well-broken, alkaline soil in full sun or semi-shade.

Parts used: leaves and stems; roots peeled and dried quickly, and powdered or fermented.

Related species: *R. peregrina* (wild madder): similar plant, though coarser in appearance, producing a paler red dye.

Rumex rugosus, syn. *R. acetosa* (Polygonaceae)
🐚 **Common Sorrel**

common sorrel

French sorrel

Description: leafy perennial with thin vertical rootstock, and basal clumps of thick shiny, arrow-shaped leaves. Leafy slender flower stems in early summer, slightly branching to 4 ft, bear loose spikes of small red-brown flowers. Grows wild in damp fields and waste land.

Uses: popular, sharply flavored pot herb since ancient Egyptian times, widely used by medieval apothecaries. Cooling and blood-cleansing, often taken as a spring tonic tea. Leaves made into poultices for acne and other skin complaints, and if picked very young can be eaten raw or cooked, notably in sorrel soup; juice of leaves will curdle milk and has also been used as a stain remover ('salts of sorrel'). Roots make a bitter tonic and a treatment for diarrhoea. **Caution:** leaves are high in oxalic acid and should be eaten sparingly; handling them may cause skin irritations.

Cultivation: sow in spring, thinning seedlings to 12 in apart, or divide roots in autumn. Grow in rich, moist soil, and keep well watered. Gather leaves frequently and remove flower stems to extend cropping.

Parts used: young leaves and buds, picked before flowering, and used fresh or frozen; roots fresh in summer.

Related species: *R. acetosella* (sheep sorrel, red sorrel): small smooth arrow-shaped leaves, piquant in salads or less sour cooked.

R. alpinus (monk's rhubarb): broad leaves, and thick creeping rhizome used in infusion as a treatment for constipation.

R. crispus (curled dock, yellow dock): tall with large, wavy leaves, used for skin complaints; root is laxative, powdered to make mouthwash and gargle; stems stewed like rhubarb; seeds ground and used in baking.

R. patientia (herb patience, sorrel-dock): tall and branched, leaves with low acidity, can be used as spinach substitute.

R. scutatus (French sorrel, round-leaved sorrel): short leafy plant, low in oxalic acid, used as a salad ingredient and pot herb.

R. vesicarius (ruby dock, wild hops): thick broad leaves and tall, bright red flowers; leaves popular vegetable with Bedu, young shoots can be added to salads.

Ruta graveolens (Rutaceae)
🌿 **Rue**
herb of grace

Description: semi-evergreen perennial shrub with woody base and branching stems up to 3 ft. Powerfully aromatic green or blue-green leaves divided into a number of spatulate leaflets, dotted with shiny oil glands. Loose racemes of small pungent yellow or yellowish-green flowers appear in summer. Found wild on dry, rocky limestone soils; cultivated in gardens as an ornamental shrub, often in blue, gold or variegated forms.

Uses: ancient medicinal herb, formerly used as an antidote to poisoning and a talisman against witchcraft. A favourite Arab herb, the only one to be blessed by Mohammed; leaves used homeopathically to treat phlebitis and varicose veins, and herbally for epilepsy, nervous complaints and uterine disorders. Essential oil used in perfumery and cosmetics; small amounts of the pungent foliage used for flavoring foods and alcoholic drinks. **Caution:** to be taken internally only under medical supervision, and used externally with care as allergic skin reactions are possible.

Cultivation: sow in a seedbed outdoors in spring, or take cuttings in late summer, and plant in full sun in well-drained soil with a little lime.

Parts used: leaves from flowering plant, fresh or dried in shade.

Salvia officinalis (Labiatae)
🌿 **Sage**

Description: variable evergreen perennial shrub, with strong taproot, and square woody, branching stems up to 2 ft 6 in, gray and woolly when young. Gray-green, pebbly-textured soft leaves are oblong or lanceolate, and finely toothed. Whorls of violet-blue flowers appear in spikes in summer. Found wild on hillsides and grassland on chalk in warm regions; widely cultivated as a pot herb in Mediterranean countries; popular herb garden shrub with numerous forms and decorative varieties, some gold or variegated. Best culinary sages are the plain narrow-leaved and non-flowering broad-leaved types.

Uses: an ancient herb, popular as a potent condiment for meat, fish, Mediterranean dishes, English Sage Derby cheese, and as a basis for sage tea, taken to counteract sweating. Infusion used to treat depression, nervous anxiety and liver disorders; homeopathic preparations given for circulation and menopausal problems. Leaves are also antiseptic, used in gargles for laryngitis and tonsillitis,

common sage

variegated sage

and as a mouth freshener and tooth cleanser. Essential oil used in perfumery.

Cultivation: grow in well-drained, rich soil, in full sun and with shelter from cold winds. Propagate from cuttings in spring and summer, or by layering (mounding for older bushes). Nip off points of shoots to induce bushy growth, and renew every 4-5 years as shrubs become leggy.

Parts used: leaves fresh, or dried in shade, picked before flowering for herbal use or when in flower for oil distillation.

clary sage

(Continued)

*(**Sage** continued)*

Related species: *S. azurea*: large blue-flowered perennial shrub, used in Mexico as a herbal panacea.

S. sclarea (clary sage): biennial with white, blue or pink flowers; leaves infused as a gargle and skin healer; source of muscatel oil for flavoring and perfumery.

S. viridis, syn. *S. horminum* (clary): annual, very similar to clary sage and similar uses; often grown as a flowering bedding plant.

S. horminoides (wild clary), *S. verbenaca*: purple-flowered species with jagged, toothed leaves and red stems; uses similar to clary sage.

S. fruticosa, syn. *S. triloba* (three-lobed sage): large perennial with lobed leaves, grown in Mediterranean countries for making the popular sage tea.

S. rutilans (pineapple sage): tender perennial with scarlet flowers in autumn and winter; fresh leaves add strong pineapple flavoring to desserts and drinks.

Sambucus nigra (Caprifoliaceae)

(Common) Elder (Berry)

Description: deciduous shrub or small tree with roughly fissured bark and numerous straight branches, up to about 30 ft. Leaves pungent and dull green, with 5-7 elliptical leaflets; red flowering stems bear broad, flat-topped heads of small white, fragrant flowers in midsummer, followed by numerous edible purple-black berries. Found wild in hedgerows, woods and built-up areas; commercially cultivated on a local scale; ornamental varieties (white, gold, cut-leaf) frequently grown in gardens.

Uses: legendary tree, long held to be guardian over all other herbs, with numerous virtues according to the part used. Leaves are an effective insect repellent, and soothing in ointments for skin complaints. Flowers soothe the eyes, are added to cosmetics, make a calming tea, and are popular for their sweet fragrance in drinks and fruit dishes. Fruits are used in cordials, syrups and preserves; medicinally to induce sweating and to treat coughs, colds, catarrh and throat infections; and as a blue-purple dye. Bark is an old treatment for epilepsy, and (together with the leaves) is laxative; root used for kidney ailments.

Cultivation: usually harvested as a wild plant, but may be grown in almost any soil and position (variegated forms best positioned in full sun for maximum color). Propagate by hardwood cuttings, easily rooted outdoors in autumn, or by suckers.

Parts used: leaves, flowers and fruits, fresh or dried; root and bark gathered as needed.

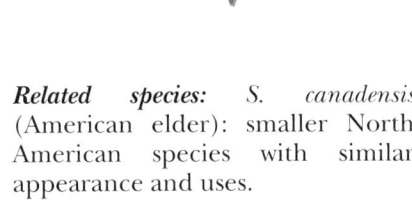

Related species: *S. canadensis* (American elder): smaller North American species with similar appearance and uses.

S. ebulus (dwarf elder, danewort): dwarf, strong-smelling perennial with creeping rhizomes, otherwise similar to common elder; used homeopathically for dropsy; berries give a blue dye; bark and flowers purgative (berries dangerously so).

S. racemosa (red-berries elder): small tree with more pointed leaves, flowers in early dense clusters, and scarlet berries in summer; purgative oil extracted from the seeds.

Santolina chamaecyparissus, syn.
S. incana (Compositae)

Santolina
cotton lavender

Description: pungent evergreen perennial shrub with branched white stems up to 20 in, silver-gray filamentous leaves, toothed along the edges. Fragrant small, bright yellow flowers like hard round buttons appear in midsummer. Grows wild in dry rocky places and warm soils; popular in gardens as an ornamental shrub and dwarf hedging plant.

Uses: grown and used since classical Greek times as a vermifuge and moth repellent. Infusion of leaves used as a rub for rheumatism and painful joints; flowers make a tonic tea. Perhaps most popular today as a decorative hedging plant for parterres and knot gardens.

Cultivation: grow in well-drained, light soil in full sun. Propagate by layering, or root cuttings with a heel in autumn or spring outdoors or in a cold frame. Clip hedges to shape in spring, and again at flowering time if only foliage is important.

Parts used: leaves before flowering, dried and stripped from stalks; flowers.

Related species: S. neapolitana (Italian lavender): taller plant with very feathery gray foliage and pale lemon-yellow flowers; similar uses.

Satureja hortensis (Labiatae)

Summer Savory
bean herb

Description: hairy aromatic annual with tough straggly or erect stems, up to 18 in. Long, dark green leaves, leathery and pointed, and lilac-pink or white flowers in small spikes from the leaf axils in late summer. Grows wild in dry, light soils and on rocky hillsides on chalk; locally cultivated for commercial use; popular garden herb.

summer savory

Uses: culinary herb whose use dates back to the early Romans; potent flavoring enhances all others in the same way as salt. Used sparingly in meat dishes and stuffings, with peas, beans and cabbage to improve their digestibility, and liqueurs. Infusion of leaves treats gastric upsets, indigestion and loss of appetite; tea is tonic. Spreading flowering shoots between clothing repels moths.

Cultivation: sow seeds in spring where plants are to grow, in well-drained soil in full sun. Species is sensitive to cold: delay sowing until the worst frosts are past, or grow the hardier winter savory. Plants self-seed freely.

Parts used: leaves gathered before flowering, fresh or dried in shade; flowering shoots fresh or dried.

winter savory

Related species: S. montana (winter savory): semi-evergreen bushy and woody perennial shrub, with smaller pink or white flowers and a slightly stronger flavor; commercially cropped for essential oil; other uses similar.

Scabiosa arvensis, syn. *Knautia arvensis* (Dipsaceae)

🐌 **Field Scabious**

blue buttons, pincushion flower

Description: evergreen perennial, with short rootstock and creeping stolons, long indented leaves. Bristly stem, up to 3 ft, bears flat heads of mauve flowers in late summer, followed by densely hairy seedheads.

Uses: infusion of roots treats cuts, sores, abrasions and itching; whole herb used as a remedy for dandruff. Homeopathically used for eczema and skin disorders.

Cultivation: sow in trays in autumn or spring, divide roots in spring or take cuttings of short side shoots. Grow in full sun in fertile, well-drained soil.

Parts used: whole flowering herb including roots, fresh or dried; roots dug in autumn, fresh or dried.

Related species: *Succisa pratensis,* syn. *Scabiosa pratensis* (devil's bit, daisy fleabane): perennial with purple, blue or white flowers; root used for wounds and diarrhoea; leaves eaten raw or cooked like spinach.

Scutellaria galericulata (Labiatae)

🐌 **(Common) Skullcap**

helmet flower

Description: downy perennial with creeping rhizome; short-stalked oval pointed leaves, bluntly toothed and dark green, with red veins on underside. Stems, up to 12 in, in summer bear large slender tubular bright violet-blue flowers in pairs. Found wild in moist lowlands, especially wet meadows.

Uses: bitter tonic and digestive herb; powerful nerve tonic, used in infusion to treat depression, headaches, insomnia, irritability and similar disorders. (Out of flower, skullcap is easily confused with wood sage, *Teucrium scorodonia.*)

Cultivation: sow seeds outdoors in spring, or divide roots in spring, and grow in good moist soil in an open, sunny position.

Parts used: all green parts during flowering, fresh or dried.

Sedum acre (Crassulaceae)

🐌 **Biting Stonecrop**

wall pepper, golden-carpet, gold moss

Description: succulent mat-forming perennial shrub with sprawling stems, and erect branches up to 8 in crowded with overlapping cylindrical short green fleshy leaves, hot and peppery to the taste. Leafy stems extend in midsummer and produce bright yellow flowers, 5-petalled and star-shaped, in loose clusters. Grows wild on walls and roofs and in dry stony soils, often on lime; and in gardens as a wall, rock garden and edging plant.

Uses: plants were often grown deliberately on roofs as charms against lightning. Homeopathically used to treat piles; bruised leaves, fresh or in ointments, are soothing for wounds, abcesses, bruises and minor burns. **Caution:** slightly poisonous; internal use may cause dizziness and nausea.

Cultivation: grow in full sun in dryish, sandy soil with a little lime. Sow seeds outdoors or divide roots in spring, or scatter some of the cylindrical leaves which root freely where they fall.

Parts used: leaves, fresh or dried in warmth.

Related species: *S. reflexum* (reflexed stonecrop): long-stemmed robust perennial, with long cylindrical leaves and golden-yellow 7-petalled flowers. Fresh non-flowering shoots are often added to soups and salads, or cooked as a tangy vegetable.

Sempervivum tectorum
(Crassulaceae)
Houseleek
hen-and-chickens

Description: fleshy perennial with short-stemmed rosette of tightly packed fleshy gray-green leaves, sometimes red-tipped, arranged in a spiral. Stem elongates in summer to form a thick leafy flower stem, 8 in high, with clusters of small rose-pink star-like blooms. Grows wild on walls, roofs and rocky mountain sites; often cultivated in pots, sinks and rock gardens.

Uses: ancient magical herb, planted on roofs as an insurance against fire and lightning. Sliced or crushed leaves used to poultice stings, burns, rashes and itching skin, and to cure warts and corns. Sometimes used as a skin lotion. In some parts of Europe young leaves and shoots are eaten as a vegetable.

Cultivation: grow in full sun in crevices and mortar joints packed with a little ordinary soil, or in sinks and pots filled with gritty compost. Propagate from seeds or leaves in trays at any time.

Parts used: leaves, sliced or pulped, as needed.

Silybum marianum (Compositae)
Milk Thistle
variegated thistle, Our Lady's milk thistle, spotted thistle

Description: prickly annual or biennial, with a thick taproot and downy white, furrowed stems up to 4 ft. Leaves oblong, wavy and spiny-edged, glossy dark green with clear white veins, and flowers red-purple and thistle-like above a collar of spiny bracts in mid-summer.

Uses: the herb has had a reputation for treating liver disorders since classical Roman times, and is included in several proprietary medicines for this purpose. Used in herbal infusions and homeopathic preparations for liver and abdominal ailments. Young shoots and leaves are edible and an Arab delicacy; roots may be cooked like parsnips, and base of flowerheads in the same way as artichokes; stems can be peeled and boiled as a vegetable; seedlings eaten raw in salads.

Cultivation: sow in spring in a sunny bed where plants are to grow, and thin seedlings to 2 ft apart.

Parts used: seedlings; young leaves and shoots; flower stems just before flowering; roots after flowering; flowerheads for medicinal use, fresh or dried in thin layers in warmth.

Smyrnium olusatrum
(Umbelliferae)
Alexanders
black lovage, horse parsley

Description: pungent biennial with solid ridged stems up to 5 ft, and large shiny, dark green leaves divided into several trefoil toothed leaflets. Flowers yellow-green and glistening with nectar, in small round umbels in midsummer, followed by globular capsules of aromatic black seeds. Grows wild on rocky banks and sea cliffs.

Uses: bitter herb cultivated since early Greek times; root is diuretic, seeds a condiment, crushed leaves or their juice a soothing and healing treatment for cuts and minor abrasions. Grown as a salad and pot herb before celery became popular, with the leaves, stems, shoots and flower buds all used, sometimes after blanching, in soups and fish dishes.

Cultivation: grow in full sun in moist soil. Sow in spring and grow as an annual leaf crop, or in autumn to overwinter and produce larger stems the following year.

Parts used: young leaves; young stems, after blanching with soil or straw if preferred; roots fresh or dried; ripe seeds.

Solidago virgaurea (Compositae)

Golden Rod

Description: herbaceous perennial with a stout knotted rhizome, and downy slender leafy stems occasionally branched, up to 5 ft. Leaves narow oval or lanceolate, and toothed; flowers tiny, bright yellow and powdery, in panicles on branched spikes in late summer. Found wild in woods, hedges and the edges of fields; commonly grown as an ornamental plant in several cultivated forms.

Uses: a medieval Arab healing herb, also used by North American Indians; made into poultices for external wounds, and infusions for fevers and digestive upsets. Occurs in several proprietary medicines for kidney and bladder ailments, and used homeopathically to treat these, as well as arthritis and rheumatism.

Cultivation: sow in spring outdoors, or divide in autumn or spring, and grow in light soils in full sun or light shade. Lift, divide and replant every 3-4 years.

Parts used: green flowering plant before flowerheads fully opened, fresh or dried in shade.

Stellaria media

Common Chickweed

Description: variable fast-growing clump-forming or sprawling annual, with weak branching straggling stems, up to 18 in long, each with a single line of longitudinal hairs. Small soft, oval fleshy leaves, long-stalked and yellowish-green, and tiny white flowers with separate thin petals, at any time. A common 'weed', forming dense mats on moist, cultivated and waste ground.

Uses: an ancient pot herb; seeds found in Neolithic burial sites. Traditionally fed to domesticated birds and fowls; a bitter salad and pot herb; homeopathic remedy for rheumatism. Poultice of stems and leaves used to ease arthritis and pains of the joints, cuts, skin irritations and inflammation.

Cultivation: seldom necessary. Plants self-seed themselves all too freely in all soils and positions, especially in dry weather.

Parts used: young stems and leaves, fresh or dried.

Symphytum officinale (Boraginaceae)

Comfrey

knitbone

Description: stout rough perennial with thick brown, fleshy rootstock, and clumps of upright basal hairy leaves, long, oval and pointed. Branched stems up to 4 ft bear purple, pink or white bell-shaped flowers in forked, curled clusters in summer. Found wild in streams, ditches and other wet places; widely cultivated in selected forms for garden use.

Uses: root formerly a popular internal remedy for gastric disorders and a homeopathic treatment for ulcers. Leaves used in infusion for bronchitis, and in poultices for wounds, bruises and eczema. Young leaves and shoots were eaten as a vegetable, cooked with a change of water. Older leaves commonly used after wilting as an animal feed, for making compost and liquid fertilizer, and for mulching plants. **Caution:** absolutely not to be used internally under any circumstances – recent evidence suggests the plant is carcinogenic.

comfrey

Cultivation: divide roots in spring or autumn, or take root cuttings in spring. Plant in moist soil in sun or shade, and mulch annually with decayed manure for maximum leaf production. Lift, divide and replant every 3-4 years. May need containment.

Russian comfrey

**variegated
Russian
comfrey**

Parts used: leaves, fresh, wilted or dried; roots fresh or split lengthways and dried in sun.

Related species: *S.* x *uplandicum* (Russian comfrey): stiffly hairy, vigorous hybrid with larger leaves, cultivated for leaf production (up to 4-6 cuts per year); often found wild in dry places as an escape.

Tanacetum parthenium, syn.
Chrysanthemum parthenium,
Matricaria parthenium
(Compositae)

Feverfew

Description: robust downy perennial with branched stems up to 3 ft. Leaves yellow-green and pungent, divided into several smaller rounded leaflets. Flowers small white daisies with prominent yellow centers, in dense clusters in midsummer.

Uses: a bitter-flavored herb, long used as a tonic and to treat indigestion, but currently popular as a treatment for migraine. Leaves are made into pain-soothing poultices for limb and joint aches, and whole flowering stems are an insect repellant, keeping moths away from clothing. A popular bee plant. **Caution:** not to be taken during pregnancy; fresh leaves may cause mouth ulcers.

Cultivation: sow in spring outdoors on the surface and water in, or take cuttings in summer. Grow in dry, well-drained soil in full sun. Plants self-seed very easily.

Parts used: leaves or whole green flowering plant, fresh or dried in shade.

Related species: *T. vulgare,* syn. *Chrysanthemum vulgare* (tansy): pungent perennial, with feathery dark green leaves and flat heads of yellow button-like flowers; an old strewing herb, insect repellent (companion plant to ward off aphids) and vermifuge; crushed leaves used to treat bruises and varicose veins; leaves once added to lamb dishes and spring puddings.

Taraxacum officinale agg.
(Compositae)

Dandelion

blowball

Description: complex group of perennials with long, stout taproots, and milky sap. Flowers on hollow stems, often reddish and downy near the top, up to 18 in; large, sweet-scented and yellow, in late spring to early autumn, followed by fluffy heads of numerous seeds, each with a parasol of white hairs to aid wind distribution.

Uses: leaves are a diuretic; dried to make tonic teas; added to herbal beer; blanched for salads. Flowers used in wines, schnapps, pancakes and in Arab baking; inside surface of flower stems soothes burns and stings (also stains skin). Roots roasted as a coffee substitute, cooked in Japanese cuisines, and give a magenta dye (with the leaves they produce brown dyes). Medicinally, given for gall-bladder and liver complaints.

Cultivation: often gathered from the wild, but may be grown as an annual by sowing in full sun in spring, barely covering seeds.

Parts used: leaves fresh or dried in warmth; flowers when fully opened in sun; roots dug in summer for medicinal use, or autumn for drying and grinding for coffee.

Related species: *T. kok-saghyz* (Russian dandelion): similar Russian wild plant, with rich milky sap, producing latex, used together with roots of *Scorzonera tau-saghyz* to make rubber.

Microseris scapigera (Australian dandelion): similar plant with larger flowers and stout yam-like root used as a vegetable by Aborigines.

Teucrium chamaedrys (Labiatae)

🐌 **Wall Germander**

Description: semi-evergreen perennial with purplish stems, sprawling or upright to 12 in. Leaves oval with rounded teeth; flowers dark lilac-purple, pink or white, in summer.

Uses: leaves used in tonic teas, wines and liqueurs, and for treating digestive and gall-bladder disorders. Plants used for edging and hedges in herb and knot gardens.

Cultivation: sow seeds in spring outdoors, take cuttings in summer, or divide plants in autumn. Grow in well-drained soil with a little lime. Clip hedges in spring and again in midsummer.

Parts used: whole flowering plant, fresh or dried in shade.

Related species: T. fruticans (tall germander): larger plant with white stems, blue-green leaves and large blue flowers.

T. scorodonia (wood sage, wood germander): pebbly sage-like leaves and yellow flowers, smelling faintly of garlic, prefers acid soils in shade; leaves used to heal and dry wounds, and in teas inhaled for throat and sinus problems.

Thlaspi arvense (Cruciferae)

🐌 **Field Pennycress**

Description: strong-smelling annual with branched stem to 18 in, oval leaves, often clasping the stem. Small white flowers in spikes appear in spring and summer, followed by pods containing black seeds. Grows wild in waste places, and sometimes a troublesome 'weed' of arable ground.

Uses: finely chopped leaves have a spicy flavor like watercress, and are used in salads and cooked dishes. Seeds were once ground and used as a mustard.

Cultivated: rarely necessary, but may be sown *in situ* in spring in fertile soil.

Parts used: leaves and young shoots before flowering; seeds dried in the sun and ground.

Related species: T. alliaceum (garlic pennycress): similar plant, with earlier flowers, narrow seedpods and scent of garlic, similar uses.

Thymus vulgaris (Labiatae)

🐌 **Common Thyme**
garden thyme

Description: variable aromatic perennial evergreen shrub with gnarled thin, square stems, woody at the base, prostrate or upright to 12 in. Leaves small, elliptical and gray-green, paler beneath; small flowers in summer, lilac or white, fragrant and popular with bees. Found wild on warm, dry rocky banks and heaths; widely grown commercially for the leaves and essential oil; favourite culinary and hedging herb in gardens, with numerous decorative and variegated forms.

Uses: popular since classical times, thyme has a number of important uses. Leaves make a tonic and stimulating tea, used to treat digestive complaints and respiratory disorders, especially for loosening mucus. Antiseptic and vermifuge essential oil (thymol) added to disinfectants, toothpaste, perfumes, toiletries and liqueurs. A culinary herb with a powerful flavor, thyme is added sparingly to bouquets garnis, stuffings and savory dishes.

common thyme

Cultivation: sow seeds or take cuttings in summer; divide plants in spring, or layer older bushes by mounding. Plant in very well drained soil in full sun. Clip after flowering and again in autumn; replace every 4-5 years, and in cold climates protect in winter, grow in containers or as a hedge.

lemon thyme

caraway thyme

wild thyme

Parts used: leaves and flowering tips, fresh or dried in sun.

Related species: *T. capitatus* (cone-head thyme): large-flowered species, grown commercially for essential oil production.

T. x *citriodora* (lemon thyme): light green species with pink flowers and strong lemon scent.

T. herba-barona (caraway thyme); arching stems rooting at tips, bronze-green leaves, strong caraway flavor.

T. mastichinus: gray-green leaves and pink flowers; widely grown in Spain for flavoring, marinades and as essential accompaniment to olives.

T. serpyllum (wild thyme, mother of thyme): very hardy, mat-forming species with late red-purple flowers and mild flavor; ideal for herb lawns; reputation as a herb for women's ailments.

Trifolium pratense (Leguminosae)
🐦 Red Clover

Description: short-lived perennial often grown as an annual, with branching roots, and arching stems, up to 20 in. Leaves long-stemmed and trefoil. Flowers pink-mauve in summer and autumn.

Uses: dried flowers produce a volatile oil and a soothing tea for promoting sleep; taken medicinally as an expectorant for respiratory disorders, and to treat skin problems such as eczema and psoriasis. Externally, an infusion soothes burns and sores. Flowers also make a good wine and yield a yellow dye.

Cultivation: sow in spring (rub the seeds with sandpaper to improve germination) in free-draining, slightly alkaline soil in rows or patches.

Parts used: flowerheads, fresh or dried in shade.

Related species: *T. alexandrinum* (berseem, Egyptian clover): very tall white fodder crop grown in Egypt and Middle East.

T. amabile (Aztec clover): Mexican and South American species, eaten as a pot herb mixed with cereals.

T. hybridum (alsike clover): small white-flowered hybrid grown as fodder and green manure in cold regions and on wet acid soils.

T. repens (white clover, Dutch clover): creeping, drought-resistant perennial with larger leaves and fragrant white or pinkish flowers liked by bees; numerous cultivated forms.

Tropaeolum majus (Tropaeolaceae)
🐦 Nasturtium

Description: South American perennial grown in temperate climates as an annual, with creeping or climbing stems to 10 ft. Leaves bright green or blue-green. Flowers orange, sometimes red or yellow, in summer and autumn, followed by spherical fruits, first green and then brown, containing three large seeds.

Uses: antiseptic and digestive herb, also used to treat respiratory and urinary disorders; seeds are a vermifuge, and crushed for use in poultices for boils and sores. Leaves are edible and used in salads, the flowers as a garnish, and both seeds and flower buds are pickled for their pungent mustard-like flavor.

Cultivation: sow spring or early summer where plants are to grow, or in pots for transplanting after frosts cease. Grow in full sun with shelter from wind, in rich soil for leaf crops, poorer dry ground for flowers and seeds.

Parts used: leaves fresh or dried; flowers; seeds while green, or when ripe for grinding as seasoning.

Tussilago farfara (Compositae)
🌿 **Coltsfoot**
coughwort, horse-hoof

Description: robust herbaceous perennial with white, scaly creeping stolons, and pale red downy, scaly stems, up to 12 in, bearing golden-yellow dandelion-like flowers that open in sun in early spring. Sturdy long-stemmed fragrant leaves follow in late spring from basal clumps, rounded or heart-shaped, irregularly toothed and up to 12 in in diameter, pale beneath with a network of clear veins. A wild plant of ditches, moist banks, waste places and loamy soils.

Uses: leaves are an important cough remedy for bronchitis and laryngitis, commonly added to herbal smoking mixtures. Both leaves (after crushing the veins) and flowers can be used in poultices for sores and ulcers; root is boiled to make coltsfoot rock or candy. Flowers are made into wine, and mature leaves can be dried and burnt to an ash used as a salt substitute. **Caution:** roots contain similar substances to comfrey, and may be equally dangerous if taken internally.

Cultivation: usually gathered from the wild, but seeds may be sown in moist soil in summer, or plants divided in autumn or used for root cuttings in winter. Plant where exposed to sunlight for most of the day. In some soils may become invasive.

Parts used: flowers before fully open, fresh or dried in shade; leaves in summer, fresh or cut up and dried in shade.

Urtica dioica (Urticaceae)
🌿 **Stinging Nettle**

Description: stinging perennial with branching roots, and bristly stems sprawling or erect up to 6 ft. Leaves covered in stinging hairs; tiny yellow-green flowers, females hanging like catkins, males in spikes in summer and autumn.

Uses: young shoots and leaves widely used in spring soups and as a green vegetable, and added to beer. Older leaves laxative in infusion, expectorant and styptic. Made into hair restorers and used homeopathically to treat skin ailments. Stems fibers are strong enough for linen weaving, papermaking and spining into ropes. Foliage is a commercial source of chlorophyll and an effective compost activator. **Caution:** handle with care, as the formic acid injected by serious stings may cause recurrent 'nettle rash'.

Cultivation: rarely necessary, but seeds may be sown in summer in fertile soil, or roots can be divided in spring.

Parts used: leaves gathered before flowering, fresh or dried in sun.

Related species: *U. breweri*, *U. thunbergiana*: North American and Japanese species respectively.

U. urens (annual nettle, burning nettle): smaller plant with reddish stems and small oval deep green leaves; similar uses.

Valeriana officinalis (Valerianaceae)
🌿 **Valerian**
garden heliotrope, cat's valerian

Description: deciduous perennial with strong-smelling branching roots, and stout tubular furrowed stems, up to 4 ft. Leaves bright green and pinnate, with 2-10 pairs of shiny oval leaflets, pointed and toothed. Small white or pink flowers in branching terminal clusters in summer. Grows wild in ditches, woods and fertile grassland.

Uses: mildly sedative and antispasmodic, used to treat tension, anxiety, insomnia, migraine and nervous ailments, as well as colic and cramp; externally in infusion for eye problems. Attractive to cats. An occasional culinary flavoring. **Caution:** large doses or extended use may lead to addiction.

Cultivation: sow in spring where plants are to grow, or separate stolons in autumn and plant in moist borders or beside pools. Tolerates full sun or deep shade; plants benefit from an annual dressing of manure.

Parts used: roots at least 2 years old and gathered after leaves fall, used fresh or dried in shade.

Related species: *V. celtica* (nard, spike): prostrate plant with brownish-yellow flowers, grown in rock gardens.

V. edulis: North American species with large tapering roots, occasionally cooked as a root vegetable.

V. phu (Cretan spikenard): white-flowered species with ornamental golden garden form; similar uses.

Veratrum viride (Liliaceae)
❧ **Green False Hellebore**
American white hellebore, itchweed, Indian poke

Description: statuesque clump-forming perennial with strong, thick roots, rosette of broad elliptical pleated or ribbed leaves. Hairy, robust stems up to 5 ft bear branched spikes of pale green or greenish-white 6-petalled star-like flowers in summer. A wild plant of moist grassy places on hills and mountain pastures (not to be confused with *Helleborus viridis*, green hellebore).

Uses: handsome flowering plant for a prominent position, anti-parasitic; used by North American Indians as an arrow poison, and by the pharmaceutical industry in preparations for reducing blood pressure. **Caution:** highly toxic and not for home preparation.

Cultivation: divide roots in autumn or spring, or sow seeds in trays of peaty soil in a cool greenhouse in spring (seeds take several months to germinate). Grow in moist semi-shade.

Parts used: roots dug in autumn, cut in pieces and dried in sun or warmth.

Related species: *V. album* (white hellebore, langwort, false helleborine): similar plant with yellowish-green flowers with similar uses; roots dried and ground into 'hellebore powder', an insecticide.

Verbena officinalis (Verbenaceae)
❧ **Vervain**

Description: hairy branching perennial with woody rootstock, and slender rough angular stems up to 3 ft, bearing long sparse 3-lobed leaves, dull grayish-green and toothed. Small lilac flowers in thin stiff spikes in late summer. Found wild in hedges, waysides and dry barren places; commonly cultivated in France and other European countries.

Uses: ancient herb popular with druids as a panacea, and used in the Middle Ages to ward off plague. Used homeopathically for dropsy; medicinally to treat rheumatism, and stomach and liver disorders. Tea is a stimulant, and relieves fevers and nervous tension. Externally used for sores and skin problems, and for eye complaints.

Cultivation: sow in spring or autumn on the surface of well-drained soil in full sun; lightly press or water in the seeds and thin seedlings to 12 in apart.

Parts used: green flowering plant, fresh or dried in sun or warmth.

Veronica officinalis (Scrophulariaceae)
❧ **(Heath) Speedwell**
fluellen

Description: hairy prostrate mat-forming perennial, with stems creeping and rooting at nodes or erect to 12 in. Small rough leaves in opposite pairs, oval and finely toothed; flowering shoots from leaf axils, in summer bearing bright lilac-blue flowers with a white eye, in clusters. Grows wild in pastures and woods, and on dry slopes and heaths on acid soils.

Uses: a medieval healing herb, still used in a tonic tea ('Swiss tea') for liver, digestive and general intestinal complaints. Fresh juice used for skin ailments, for which there is also a homeopathic preparation. Cultivated as an ornamental ground-cover plant in the garden.

Cultivation: sow in spring or divide plants in early summer, and grow in rich, fertile soil in full sun. Water freely in dry weather, and replace plants every 4-5 years.

Parts used: whole green flowering plant, fresh or dried in shade or a warm room.

Related species: *V. beccabunga* (brooklime, water pimpernel): fleshy aquatic perennial with small, bright blue flowers found beside streams and in other wet places; popular salad plant high in vitamin C, and a very mild purgative.

Veronicastrum virginicum, syn. *Veronica virginica* (culver's root, bowman's root): very tall slender blue- or white-flowered perennial, once used by Shakers as a digestive. **Caution:** highly purgative.

Vinca minor (Apocynaceae)
🐌 **Lesser Periwinkle**

Description: evergreen perennial, with stems prostrate and rooting at leaf nodes, and leafy flowering stems erect to 2 ft. Leaves glossy and oval, flowers pale blue with lighter centers, or white, on hollow stalks in early summer.

Uses: used as a gargle for sore throats, as a styptic and astringent for wounds, sores and ulcers, and in a tea to reduce blood pressure and hypertension. **Caution:** large amounts may be toxic, leading to circulatory disorders.

Cultivation: divide in spring or take stem cuttings in autumn, and grow in fertile moist soils with a little lime.

Parts used: green flowering plant in spring, fresh or dried.

Related species: Vinca major (greater periwinkle, blue buttons): longer-stalked leaves and stems rooting only at the tips.

Viola tricolor (Violaceae)
🐌 **Wild Pansy**
heartsease, field pansy, johnny jump-up

Description: variable annual or short-lived perennial, almost evergreen, with hollow stems sprawling or erect to 8 in. Leaves oval and indented. Flowers yellow with purple and white markings, from spring to autumn, followed by capsules filled with shiny, light brown seeds, splitting into three segments when ripe.

Uses: renowned mild heart tonic, used to treat high blood pressure, indigestion and colds; cleanses blood and induces perspiration. Also used to treat dropsy and rheumatic conditions, and for skin disorders such as acne and eczema.

Cultivation: sow spring or summer where plants are to grow; press seeds into soil but leave uncovered. Surplus seedlings may be transplanted to any position in semi-shade. Plants self-seed freely. Cut back leggy plants to induce bushy growth and further flowers.

Parts used: green flowering herb and root, fresh or dried in shade.

Related species: V. odorata (sweet violet): trailing stoloniferous perennial with sweet-scented purple, white or pink flowers; ancient strewing herb and commercial crop for perfume industry; leaves and flowers used to treat coughs, catarrh and respiratory disorders; flowers crystallized.

V. sororia, syn. *V. papilionacea*: North American purple-flowered wild species with several cultivated forms; used by Indians for colds and headaches.

Vitex agnus-castus (Verbenaceae)
🐌 **Chaste Berry**
Indian spice, monk's pepper, chaste tree

Description: aromatic shrub or small tree up to 20 ft, with palmate leaves divided into narrow leaflets on gray, downy shoots. Small violet fragrant flowers in dense trusses growing up to 12 in long in autumn, followed in warm climates by purple-black berries. Found wild on light, stony soils in southern Europe; cultivated as a garden ornamental, sometimes with white flowers.

Uses: an ancient Greek herb thought to guarantee chastity, now used to regulate female hormonal activity. Also reputed to be a male anaphrodisiac; used as symbolic strewing herb in Italian monasteries. Seeds are used as a peppery condiment, slender branches in basketwork.

Cultivation: sow seeds in spring, layer in summer, or take cuttings under glass in autumn. Grow in well-drained, light soil, in full sun, and against a warm sheltered wall in temperate regions.

Parts used: fruits picked in autumn, fresh or dried in shade.

Related species: Vitex negundo (Chinese chaste tree): medium shrub with square stems and lavender flowers in late summer.

Right: *A fruitful, healthy herb garden – the results of only a little research and planning.*

BEE AND BUTTERFLY HERBS

• anise	• bergamot
• betony	• broom
• chicory	• chives
• comfrey	• coltsfoot
• evening primrose	• fennel
• hyssop	• lavender
• lemon balm	• meadowsweet
• mint	• rosemary
• sage	• self-heal
• thyme	• valerian
• yarrow	

AN ESSENTIAL HERB COLLECTION

• basil – a tender annual

• bay – grown as a small trained specimen

• chives – for edging

• dill – an annual

• fennel – bulky and tall

• French tarragon – tall, best in a container

• lemon balm – a herbaceous perennial

• marjoram – shrubby

• mint – best in a pot

• parsley – ideal for edging

• rosemary – a bushy shrub

• sweet cicely – American (*Osmorrhiza longistylis*) or European (*Myrrhis odorata*)

• thyme – mats of evergreen foliage

• winter savory – short evergreen shrub

HERBS FOR FIRST AID

Part of the herb garden can be reserved for a selection of plants to provide help in emergencies; most can be used fresh in teas, compresses and infusions.

• aloe vera – grow as a pot plant and use a broken leaf to relieve sunburn

• lavender – use as an infusion for coughs, colds and headaches

• pot marigold – make a poultice from the flowers for burns and stings

• witch hazel – use in compresses for bruises and bleeding

• German chamomile – can be taken as a tea for insomnia

• lemon balm – infuse for digestive and menstrual upsets

• St John's wort – use as a compress for cuts and small wounds

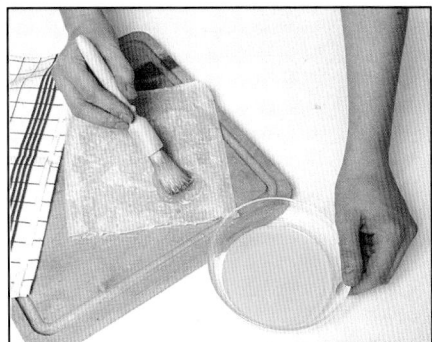 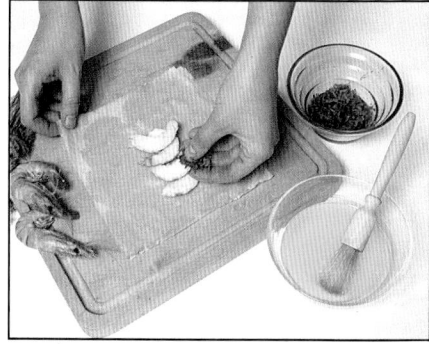

Tiger Shrimp in Filo with Mint, Dill and Lime

Another wonderful combination – the mint, dill and lime blend together to make a magical concoction that will delight everyone who tries it.

SERVES 4

4 large sheets filo pastry

75 g/3 oz/¹⁄₃ cup butter

16 large tiger shrimp, cooked and shelled

1 tbsp chopped fresh mint, plus a little more to garnish

1 tbsp chopped fresh dill

juice of 1 lime, plus another lime cut into wedges

1 Keep the sheets of filo pastry covered with a dry, clean cloth to keep them moist. Cut one sheet of filo pastry in half widthwise and brush both halves with melted butter. Place one half on top of the other.

2 Preheat the oven to 450°F. Cut eight of the tiger shrimp in half down the back of the shrimp and remove any black parts.

3 Place four prawns in the center of the filo pastry and sprinkle a quarter of the mint, dill and lime juice over the top. Fold over the sides, brush with butter and roll up to make a bundle.

4 Repeat with the other ingredients and place the bundles join side down, on a greased cookie sheet. Bake for 10 minutes or until golden. Serve with lime wedges, tiger shrimp and mint.

Camembert, Chervil and Plum Profiteroles

Most people are familiar with chocolate profiteroles, but this savory version is just as delicious and makes an attractive starter.

SERVES 8

1¼ cups water

⅔ cup butter, cubed

1½ cups plain flour

2 tsp mustard powder

1 tsp powdered cinnamon

4 eggs

¾ cup grated Cheddar

FILLING

1 packed cup Camembert

a little milk

1 tsp fresh chervil, chopped

6 fresh plums, stoned and finely chopped

SAUCE

10 oz can red plums

½ tsp powdered cinnamon

1 tsp chopped fresh chervil, plus a few sprigs to garnish

1 To make the profiteroles, put the water into a saucepan and add the butter. Gently melt the butter, then bring to the boil. As soon as this happens, sieve in the flour, mustard powder and cinnamon. Beat hard with a wooden spoon until the mixture comes away from the sides of the pan.

2 Leave to cool for 10 minutes, then beat in the eggs, one at a time. Add the grated Cheddar, and beat until glossy. Use a large nozzle to pipe blobs about 1 in across on a greased cookie sheet. Bake at 400°F for 20 minutes. Cool on a wire rack.

3 Chop the Camembert in small pieces and put in a food processor. Add a little milk and the chervil, and blend to a smooth paste. Remove from the food processor and add the fresh plums.

4 Also make the sauce while the pastries are cooling. Drain the canned plums and pit them if necessary. Add them to the cinnamon and chervil in the food processor and blend to a fairly smooth purée.

5 Assemble the profiteroles by halving them and placing some of the Camembert mixture inside. Place the profiteroles on individual plates and dust with a little cinnamon. Serve the sauce separately.

Pork, Thyme and Water Chestnut Filo Bundles

Filo pastry is easy to use and delicious – the light, crisp wrapping makes a simple recipe into a celebration.

MAKES 8

1 tbsp sunflower oil, plus more for frying

1 tsp fresh grated ginger

10 oz pork fillet, finely chopped

6 scallions, chopped

1 cup chopped mixed mushrooms

½ cup chopped canned bamboo shoots

12 water chestnuts, finely chopped

2 tsp cornstarch

1 tbsp soy sauce

2 tsp anchovy paste

2 tsp fresh thyme, chopped

salt and pepper

8 large sheets filo pastry

scant 2 tbsp butter, melted

1 Heat the oil and fry the ginger for a few seconds and then add the pork. Stir well and cook until color changes. Add the scallions and mushrooms and cook until tender. Add the bamboo shoots and water chestnuts and cook quickly.

2 In a small bowl, mix the cornstarch with the soy sauce and anchovy paste. Add to the pan and stir well. Add the chopped thyme, season with salt and pepper, and cook until thickened.

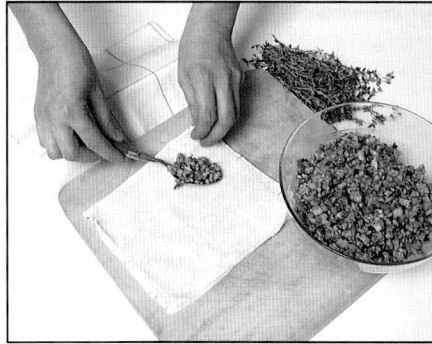

3 Take a sheet of filo pastry and fold in half to make a square. Place two tablespoonfuls of filling across one corner and fold the corner over, then fold in the sides. Brush the folded sides lightly with a little melted butter to help the pastry stick. Complete the roll, and place it join side down on a cloth, then fold the cloth over the top to cover it. Finish all the rolls, putting each one in the cloth as it is made.

4 Heat some oil for semi-deep frying, and fry 2-3 rolls at a time until evenly browned. Drain on absorbent paper and serve hot.

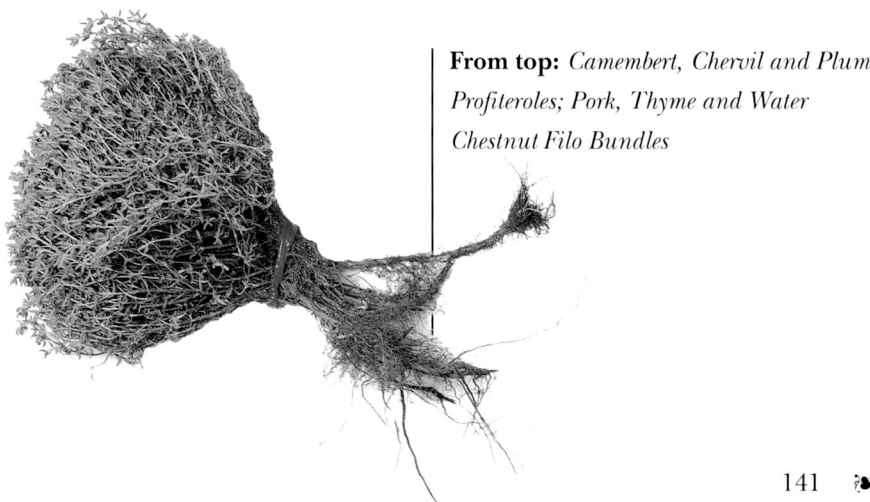

From top: *Camembert, Chervil and Plum Profiteroles; Pork, Thyme and Water Chestnut Filo Bundles*

Lamb Pie, with Pear, Ginger and Mint Sauce

Cooking lamb with fruit is an idea taken from traditional Persian cuisine. The ginger and mint add bite to the mild flavors.

SERVES 6

1 boned mid-loin of lamb, 2 lb after
  boning

salt and pepper

8 large sheets filo pastry

scant 2 tbsp butter

STUFFING

1 tbsp butter

1 small onion, chopped

1 cup coarsely crumbled whole wheat
  bread

grated rind of 1 lemon

³/₄ cup drained canned pears from a
  14 oz can, roughly chopped
  (rest of can, and juice, used for
  sauce)

¼ tsp ground ginger

1 small egg, beaten

skewers, string and large needle to
  make roll

SAUCE

rest of can of pears, including juice

2 tsp finely chopped fresh mint

1 Prepare the stuffing: melt the butter in a pan and add the onion, cooking until soft. Preheat the oven to 350°F. Put the butter and onion into a mixing bowl and add the breadcrumbs, lemon rind, pears and ginger. Season lightly and add enough beaten egg to bind.

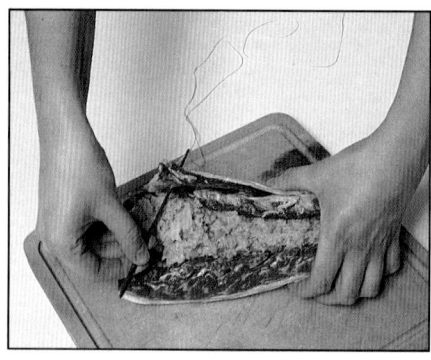

2 Spread the loin out flat, fat side down, and season. Place the stuffing along the middle of the loin and roll carefully, holding with skewers while you sew it together with string. Heat a large baking pan in the oven and brown the loin slowly on all sides. This will take 20-30 minutes. Leave to cool, and store in the refrigerator until needed.

3 Preheat the oven to 400°F. Take two sheets of filo pastry and brush with melted butter. Overlap by about 5 in to make a square. Place the next two sheets on top and brush with butter. Continue until all the pastry has been used.

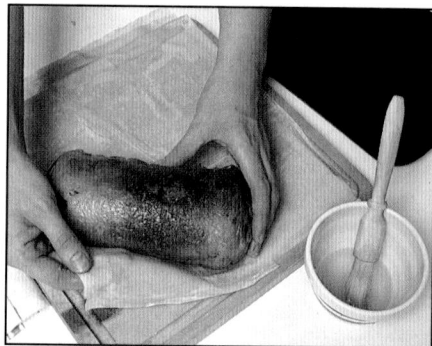

4 Place the roll of lamb diagonally across one corner of the pastry, without overlapping the sides. Fold the corner over the lamb, fold in the sides, and brush the pastry well with melted butter. Roll to the far corner of the sheet. Place join side down on a buttered baking sheet and brush all over with the rest of the melted butter. Bake for about 30 minutes or until golden brown.

5 Blend the remaining pears with their juice and the mint, and serve with the lamb.

Steak and Kidney Pie, with Mustard and Bay Gravy

This is a sharpened-up, bay-flavored version of a traditional favorite. The fragrant mustard, bay and parsley perfectly complement the flavor of the beef.

SERVES 4

1 lb puff pastry
2½ tbsp flour
salt and pepper
1½ lb rump steak, cubed
6 oz pork or lamb kidney
scant 2 tbsp butter
1 medium onion, chopped
1 tbsp made English mustard
2 bay leaves
1 tbsp chopped parsley
⅔ cup beef stock
1 egg, beaten

1 Roll out two-thirds of the pastry on a floured surface to about ⅛ in thick. Gently transfer to line a 1½ quart pie dish. Place a pie funnel in the middle.

2 Put the flour, salt and pepper in a bowl and toss the cubes of steak in the mixture. Remove all fat and skin from the kidneys, and slice thickly. Add to the steak cubes and toss well. Melt the butter in a pan and fry the onion until soft, then add the mustard, bay leaves, parsley and stock and stir well.

3 Preheat the oven to 375°F. Place the steak and kidney in the pie and add the stock mixture. Roll out the remaining pastry to a thickness of ⅛ in. Brush the edges of the pastry forming the lower half of the pie with beaten egg and cover with the second piece of pastry. Firmly press the pieces of pastry together to seal the edge, then trim. Use the trimmings to decorate the top in a leaf pattern.

4 Brush the whole pie with beaten egg and make a small hole over the top of the funnel. Bake for about 1 hour until the pastry is golden brown.

143

Turkey with Apples, Bay and Madeira

This casserole will win you many compliments without the worry of a complicated menu. The unusual apple garnish looks very attractive.

<small>SERVES 4</small>

1½ lb turkey breast fillets, cut into
  ¾ in slices

salt and pepper

4 tbsp unsalted butter, plus another
  1 tbsp for the sliced apple garnish

4 tart apples, peeled and sliced

4 tbsp Madeira or cooking sherry,
  plus another 2 tbsp for the apple
  garnish

⅔ cup chicken stock

3 bay leaves

2 tsp cornstarch

⅔ cup heavy cream

1 Season the turkey, melt 2 tbsp of the butter in a pan and fry the meat to seal it. Transfer to an ovenproof casserole. Preheat the oven to 350°F. Add the remaining 2 tbsps butter to the pan with two sliced apples, and cook gently for 1-2 minutes.

2 Add the Madeira, stock and bay leaves to the turkey and stir in. Simmer for another couple of minutes. Cover the casserole and bake for about 40 minutes.

3 Blend the cornstarch with a little of the cream, then add the rest of the cream. Add this mixture to the casserole and return to the oven for 10 minutes to allow the sauce to thicken.

4 To make the garnish, melt 1 tbsp butter in a pan and gently fry the apple slices. Add the remaining Madeira and set it alight. Once the flames have died down continue to fry the apple until it is lightly browned, and garnish the casserole with it.

Beef with Orange Herbal Mustard

The orange herbal mustard is delicious with many different dishes, including cold ham and pork pies. It gives beef a fantastic flavor. This will become a firm favorite.

SERVES 4

3 tbsp oil

1½ lb braising steak, cubed

2 cups chopped onion

1 clove garlic, peeled and crushed

2 tbsp flour

1¼ cups beef stock

**2 oranges, plus 1 more for garnish
and herbal mustard**

1 tbsp tomato paste

3 tbsp Grand Marnier

1 tbsp maple syrup

salt and pepper

1 cup sliced mushrooms

HERBAL MUSTARD

**2 tbsp mixed fresh herbs, finely
chopped, such as thyme and chives**

**juice and grated rind of half an
orange**

3 tbsp Dijon mustard

1 Heat the oil and fry the beef to seal it. Transfer to a casserole. Fry the onion and garlic, drain and add to the casserole. Add the flour to the pan and cook for 1 minute, then add the stock and bring to a boil.

2 Finely slice off the colored part of the rind of two oranges and chop into small pieces. Squeeze both oranges, and add the juice and the rind to the casserole. Add the tomato paste, Grand Marnier and maple syrup, and season to taste. Preheat the oven to 350°F.

3 Cover the casserole and cook in the oven for at least 1½ hours. Add the mushrooms and return to the oven for another 30 minutes. Serve garnished with slices from half the remaining orange and the herbal mustard described below (remember to grate the orange before cutting it up).

4 To make the herbal mustard, grate the orange rind and mix with the chopped fresh herbs. Then mix in the orange juice and the Dijon mustard. Serve with the beef in a separate dish.

Chicken Stew with Blackberries and Lemon Balm

This delicious stew combines some wonderful flavors, and the combination of red wine and blackberries gives it a dramatic appearance.

SERVES 4

4 chicken breasts, partly boned

salt and pepper

scant 2 tbsp butter

1 tbsp sunflower oil

4 tbsp flour

$^2/_3$ cup red wine

$^2/_3$ cup chicken stock

grated rind of half an orange plus 1 tbsp juice

3 sprigs lemon balm, finely chopped, plus 1 sprig to garnish

$^2/_3$ cup heavy cream

1 egg yolk

$^2/_3$ cup fresh blackberries, plus $^1/_3$ cup to garnish

1 Remove any skin from the chicken, and season the meat. Heat the butter and oil in a pan, fry the chicken to seal it, then transfer to a casserole dish. Stir the flour into the pan, then add wine and stock and bring to a boil. Add the orange rind and juice, and also the chopped lemon balm. Pour over the chicken.

2 Preheat the oven to 350°F. Cover the casserole and cook in the oven for about 40 minutes.

3 Blend the cream with the egg yolk, add some of the liquid from the casserole and stir back into the dish with the blackberries (reserving those for the garnish). Cover and cook for another 10-15 minutes. Serve garnished with the rest of the blackberries and lemon balm.

Pork and Mushrooms with Sage and Mango Chutney

The mango chutney and sage leaves add a special flavor to this traditional dish.

SERVES 4

scant 2 tbsp butter

1 tbsp sunflower oil

1$^1/_2$ lb cubed pork

6 oz onion, peeled and chopped

2 tbsp flour

1$^7/_8$ cups stock

4 tbsp white wine

salt and pepper

8 oz mushrooms, sliced

6 fresh sage leaves, finely chopped

2 tbsp mango chutney

1 fresh mango, peeled and sliced, to garnish

1 Heat the butter and oil and fry the pork in a pan to seal it. Transfer to a casserole. Fry the onion in the pan, stir in the flour and cook for 1 minute.

2 Preheat the oven to 350°F. Gradually add the stock and white wine to the onion and bring to a boil. Season well with salt and pepper, then add the mushrooms, sage leaves and mango chutney.

3 Pour the sauce mixture over the pork and cover the casserole. Cook in the oven for about 1 hour, depending on the cut of pork, until tender. Check the seasoning, garnish with mango slices, and serve with rice.

From top: *Pork and Mushrooms with Sage and Mango Chutney; Chicken Stew with Blackberries and Lemon Balm*

3 In a pan, reduce the red wine, then add the orange juice and elderberry jelly and simmer for 10 minutes. Pour over the steaks and garnish with slices of orange and parsley sprigs.

1 Pound the venison steaks a little with a meat mallet to make the meat more tender. Preheat the broiler.

2 Brush with olive oil and season with freshly ground black pepper. Broil under a high heat until done to your taste. Sprinkle with a little salt.

From top: *Venison Steaks with Elderberry and Orange; Herbed Chicken with Apricot and Pecan Potato Baskets*

153

Chicken with Sloe Gin and Juniper

 *Juniper is used in the manufacture of gin, and the reinforcement of the flavor by using both sloe gin and juniper is delicious. Sloe gin is easy to make, but can also be bought ready-made.*

SERVES 8

2 tbsp butter

2 tbsp sunflower oil

8 chicken breast fillets

12 oz carrots, cooked

1 clove garlic, peeled and crushed

1 tbsp finely chopped parsley

¼ cup chicken stock

¼ cup red wine

¼ cup sloe gin

1 tsp crushed juniper berries

salt and pepper

1 bunch basil, to garnish

1 Melt the butter with the oil in a pan, and sauté the chicken until browned on all sides.

2 In a food processor, combine all the remaining ingredients except the watercress, and blend to a smooth purée. If the mixture seems too thick add a little more red wine or water until a thinner consistency is reached.

3 Put the chicken breasts in a pan, pour the sauce over the top and cook until the chicken is cooked through – about 15 minutes. Adjust the seasoning and serve garnished with chopped fresh basil.

Duck Breasts with Red Plums, Cinnamon and Coriander

Duck breasts can be bought separately, which makes this dish very easy to prepare.

SERVES 4

4 lean duck breasts, 6 oz each, skinned

salt

2 tsp stick cinnamon, crushed

¼ cup butter

1 tbsp plum brandy (or Cognac)

1 cup chicken stock

1 cup heavy cream

pepper

6 fresh red plums, pitted and sliced

6 sprigs coriander leaves, plus some extra to garnish

1 Preheat the oven to 375°F. Score the duck breasts and sprinkle with salt. Press the crushed cinnamon on to both sides of the duck breasts. Melt half the butter in a pan and fry them on both sides to seal, then place in an ovenproof dish with the butter and bake for 6-7 minutes.

2 Remove the dish from the oven and return the contents to the pan. Add the brandy and set it alight. When the flames have died down, remove from the pan and keep warm. Add the stock and cream to the pan and simmer gently until reduced and thick. Adjust the seasoning.

3 Reserve a few plum slices for garnishing. In a pan, melt the other half of the butter and fry the plums and coriander, just enough to cook the fruit through. Slice the duck breasts and pour some sauce around each one, then garnish with slices of plum and chopped coriander.

Turkey with Fig, Orange and Mint Marmalade

Turkey is a low-fat meat that should be used all the year round, not just at Christmas. This unusual sauce gives its rather bland flavor a tremendous lift.

S<small>ERVES</small> 4

1 lb dried figs

½ bottle sweet, fruity white wine

4 turkey fillets, 6-8 oz each

1 tbsp butter

2 tbsp dark orange marmalade

10 mint leaves, finely chopped, plus a
  few more to garnish

juice of ½ lemon

salt and pepper

1 Place the figs in a pan with the wine and bring to a boil, then simmer very gently for about 1 hour. Leave to cool and refrigerate overnight.

2 Melt the butter in a pan and fry the turkey fillets until they are cooked through. Remove from the pan and keep warm. Drain any fat from the pan and pour in the juice from the figs. Bring to the boil and reduce until about ⅔ cup remains.

3 Add the marmalade, mint leaves and lemon juice, and simmer for a few minutes. Season to taste. When the sauce is thick and shiny, pour it over the meat and garnish with the figs and mint leaves.

Lamb with Mint and Lemon

Lamb has been served with mint for centuries – rightly, because it is a great combination.

SERVES 8

8 lamb steaks, 8 oz each

grated rind and juice of 1 lemon

2 cloves garlic, peeled and crushed

2 scallions, finely chopped

2 tsp finely chopped fresh mint leaves, plus some leaves for garnishing

4 tbsp extra virgin olive oil

salt and black pepper

1 Make a marinade for the lamb by mixing all the other ingredients and seasoning to taste. Place the lamb steaks in a shallow dish and cover with the marinade. Refrigerate overnight.

2 Preheat the broiler then broil the lamb under a high heat until just cooked, basting with the marinade occasionally. Turn once during cooking. Garnish with mint leaves.

Sirloin Steaks with Bloody Mary Sauce and Coriander

This cocktail of ingredients is just as successful as the well - known drink, but the alcohol evaporates in cooking, so you need not worry about a hangover.

SERVES 4

4 sirloin steaks, 8 oz each
MARINADE
2 tbsp soy sauce
4 tbsp balsamic vinegar
2 tbsp olive oil
SAUCE
2 lb very ripe tomatoes, peeled and chopped
tomato paste, if required
1/2 cup chopped onions
2 spring onions
1 tsp chopped fresh coriander
1 tsp ground cumin
1 tsp salt
1 tbsp fresh lime juice
1/2 cup beef consommé, fresh or canned
1/4 cup vodka
1 tbsp Worcester sauce

1 Lay the steaks in a shallow dish, mix the marinade ingredients together in a bowl, pour over the steaks and leave for at least a couple of hours in the refrigerator, turning once or twice.

2 If the tomatoes are not quite ripe, add a little tomato paste. Place all the sauce ingredients in a food processor and blend to a fairly smooth texture. Put in a pan, bring to a boil and simmer for about 5 minutes.

3 Remove the steaks from the marinade and place under a hot broiler. Discard the marinade. Broil the steaks under a high heat until cooked. Serve with the sauce.

Roast Pork with Sage, Marjoram and Celery Leaves

Pork is an inexpensive choice which is equally suitable for a family dinner or a celebration meal. The fruity purée makes a delicious change from the more usual plain apple sauce.

SERVES 8

6 lb joint of pork
3 tbsp fresh sage
1 tbsp fresh marjoram
3 tbsp chopped celery leaves
salt and pepper
1/4 cup cider
PURÉE
1 tbsp butter
2 eating apples
2 bananas
1 tbsp Calvados

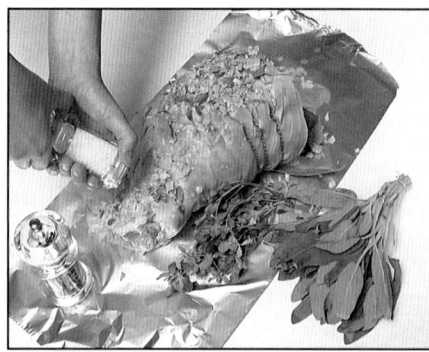

1 Preheat the oven to 315°F. Cut a large piece of foil and place the pork in the center. In a bowl mix the sage, marjoram and celery leaves together. Cover the fatty part of the pork with the herb mixture, season to taste and wrap tightly. Roast for about 1 hour.

2 Fold back the foil and baste the joint with the cider. Continue cooking for another hour until a sharp knife pressed into the thickest part produces clear juices.

3 To make the purée, peel and slice the apples and bananas, put the butter in a pan and sauté the fruit. Add the Calvados and set it alight. When the flames have died down remove the mixture from the heat, put it in the food processor and purée. Serve the pork with the purée on the side.

From top: *Sirloin Steaks with Bloody Mary Sauce and Coriander; Roast Pork with Sage, Marjoram and Celery Leaves*

Corn on the Cob in a Garlic Butter Crust

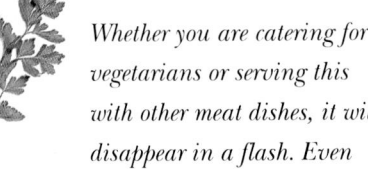

Whether you are catering for vegetarians or serving this with other meat dishes, it will disappear in a flash. Even people who are not usually keen on corn on the cob have been won over by this recipe.

SERVES 6

6 ripe cobs of corn

1 cup butter

2 tbsp olive oil

2 cloves garlic, peeled and crushed

2 tsp freshly ground black pepper

1 cup finely crumbled whole wheat bread

1 tbsp chopped parsley

1 Boil the corn cobs in salted water until tender, then leave to cool.

2 Melt the butter, and add the oil, garlic and black pepper. Pour the mixture into a shallow dish. Mix the breadcrumbs and parsley in another shallow dish. Roll the corn cobs in the melted butter mixture and then in the breadcrumbs.

3 Grill the cobs under a high grill until the breadcrumbs are golden.

OTHER GARLIC BUTTER IDEAS

• Partially cut through a French loaf at regular intervals. Spread the garlic butter mixture between the slices and bake in a moderate oven for 30 minutes.

• To make garlic crôutons, melt the garlic butter in a pan and add cubes of bread. Toss frequently over a medium heat. When golden brown add to soups or salads.

• Drizzle over chicken breasts before roasting.

Chocolate Mint Truffle Filo Parcels

These exquisite little parcels are utterly irresistible. There will be no leftovers.

18 PARCELS

1 tbsp very finely chopped mint

¾ cup ground almonds

2 oz plain chocolate, grated

2 apples, peeled and grated

4 oz crème fraîche or whole-milk
  ricotta cheese

9 large sheets filo pastry

⅓ cup butter, melted

1 tbsp confectioners' sugar

1 tbsp cocoa powder, to dust

1 Preheat the oven to 375°F. Mix the mint, almonds, chocolate, crème fraîche or ricotta and grated apple in a bowl. Cut the filo pastry sheets into 3 in squares, and cover with a cloth to stop them drying out.

2 Brush a square of filo with melted butter, lay on a second sheet, brush again, and place a spoonful of filling in the middle of the top sheet. Bring in all four corners and twist to form a purse shape. Repeat to make 18 parcels.

3 Place the filo parcels on a cookie sheet, well brushed with melted butter. Bake for approximately 10 minutes. Leave to cool and then dust with the confectioners' sugar, and then with the cocoa powder.

From left to right: *Clementines in Beaumes de Venise with Geranium; Chocolate Mint Truffle Filo Parcels*

183

Rosemary Vinegar

Flavored vinegars make a huge difference to the taste of a salad dressing. They are very simple to make, and the jars are a pretty windowsill decoration. Try the same recipe with nasturtium flowers, if you like.

ABOUT 2½ CUPS

fresh rosemary sprigs, to fill a 2½ cup measure, plus more to decorate

2½ cups white distilled vinegar

1 Fill a sterilized wide-necked bottle or jar with the sprigs of rosemary. Fill to the top with vinegar. Cover tightly and place in a sunny spot for around 4-6 weeks.

2 Filter the vinegar mixture through a coffee filter paper. Discard the rosemary. Heat the vinegar until it begins to simmer, but do not boil.

3 Wash the bottle or jar and its lid well in hot, soapy water, rinse thoroughly, and dry in a warm oven. Pour the vinegar back into it or other sterilized decorative bottles. You can add a fresh sprig or two of rosemary for decorative purposes if you wish, then seal. Store in a dark place. Use within one year.

Herb Garden Dressing

This dried mixture will keep through the winter until your herbs are growing again. It can be used to flavor salad dressings and to sprinkle over vegetables, casseroles and stews.

1 cup dried oregano

1 cup dried basil

$\frac{1}{2}$ cup dried marjoram

$\frac{1}{2}$ cup dried dill weed

$\frac{1}{2}$ cup dried mint leaves

$\frac{1}{2}$ cup onion powder

2 tbsp dry mustard

2 tsp salt

1 tbsp freshly ground black pepper

1 Mix the ingredients together and keep in a sealed jar to use as needed.

2 When making a batch of salad dressing, take 2 tbsp of the herb mixture and add it to $1\frac{1}{2}$ cups of extra virgin olive oil and $\frac{1}{2}$ cup cider vinegar. Mix thoroughly and allow to stand for 1 hour or so. Mix again and correct the seasoning before using.

185

Dill Pickles

A good pickle to have in your kitchen cupboard. It is excellent sliced onto a hamburger, served with cold meats, and in canapés and snacks. If you like, try varying the type of cucumbers used. The French are fond of tiny 'cornichons', while the traditional Northern American versions are much larger.

ABOUT 2½ QUARTS

6 small cucumbers

2 cups water

4 cups white wine vinegar

½ cup salt

3 bay leaves

3 tbsp dill seed

2 cloves garlic, slivered

dill flowerheads, to garnish

1 Slice the cucumbers into medium-thick slices. Put the water, vinegar and salt in a saucepan and boil, then remove immediately from the heat.

2 Layer the herbs and garlic between slices of cucumber in sterilized preserving jars until the jars are full, then cover with the warm salt and vinegar mixture. Leave on a sunny window sill for at least a week before using.

Parsley, Sage and Thyme Oil

Herb oils are an excellent ingredient for use in stir-fry cooking as well as salad dressings. This mixed herb combination is a good basic choice, but you can also be adventurous and try other, more exotic ingredients. Adding garlic and chillis to a herb oil produces a fiery condiment: try dribbling a tiny amount on to pasta for extra flavor.

ABOUT 2½ CUPS

2½ cups sunflower oil

½ cup chopped fresh parsley, curly or Italian

⅛ cup chopped fresh sage

¼ cup chopped fresh thyme

1 Pour the oil into a sterilized jar and add all the herbs. Cover and allow to stand at room temperature for about a week, no longer. Stir or shake occasionally during that time.

2 Then strain off the oil into a sterilized bottle and discard the used herbs. Add a fresh sprig or two for decorative purposes if you wish. Seal the jar carefully. Store, preferably in a cool place, for 6 months at the most.

Cranberry and Port Sauce with Lemon Thyme

Cranberry and port sauce is delicious served with turkey, chicken, pork or ham. Lemon thyme really sets off its unique flavor.

ABOUT 2½ CUPS

4 tbsp port

4 tbsp orange juice

½ cup sugar

8 oz fresh cranberries, picked over

1 tbsp finely grated orange rind

1 tbsp very finely chopped lemon thyme

1 Pour the port and orange juice into a saucepan and add the sugar. Place the pan over a low heat and stir frequently with a metal spoon to dissolve the sugar.

2 Transfer the mixture to a larger pan. Increase the heat a little and add the cranberries. Bring the mixture to the boil and simmer for 5 minutes, stirring occasionally, until the cranberries are just tender and the skins begin to burst.

3 Remove the pan from the heat and carefully mix in the orange rind and lemon thyme.

4 Leave the sauce to cool, then pour into sterilized glass jars and seal with waxed paper circles and cellophane lids secured with rubber bands. Add a label and decorate with short lengths of string tied around the top if you like.

Lemon and Mint Curd

Home-made lemon curd is infinitely tastier than the commercial variety. The addition of mint gives this version an interesting extra tang. Try experimenting with different types of mint. Lemon curd is best made using the freshest of ingredients. Buy fresh eggs, and try to find unwaxed lemons.

ABOUT 3 LB

6 fresh mint leaves

4 cups superfine sugar

1½ cups unsalted butter, cut into chunks

rind of 6 lemons, thinly pared, in large pieces, and their juice

8 eggs, beaten

1 Place the mint leaves and sugar in a food processor, and blend until the mint leaves are very finely chopped and combined with the sugar.

2 Put the mint sugar and all the other ingredients into a bowl and mix together.

3 Set the bowl over a pan of simmering water. Cook, whisking gently, until all the butter has melted and the sugar has dissolved. Remove the lemon rind.

4 Continue to cook in this way, stirring frequently, for 35-40 minutes or until the mixture thickens. Pour into sterilized glass jars, filling them up to the rim. Seal with waxed paper circles and cellophane lids secured with rubber bands. Add a label and tie short lengths of string around the top of the jars to decorate. This lemon curd should be used within 3 months.

From top: *Lemon and Mint Curd; Cranberry and Port Sauce with Lemon Thyme*

Rhubarb and Ginger Mint Preserve

Ginger mint is easily grown in the garden, and is just the thing to boost the flavor of rhubarb jam. Stewed rhubarb also tastes good with a little ginger mint added to the pan.

<u>ABOUT 6 LB</u>

4 lb rhubarb

1 cup water

juice of 1 lemon

2 in piece fresh ginger root, peeled

6 cups sugar

$^2/_3$ cup preserved ginger in syrup, drained and chopped

2-3 tbsp very finely chopped ginger mint leaves

1 Wash and trim the rhubarb, cutting it into small pieces about 1 in long. Place the rhubarb, water and lemon juice in a preserving pan and bring to the boil. Bruise the piece of fresh ginger root and add it to the pan. Simmer, stirring frequently, until the rhubarb is soft and then remove the ginger.

2 Add the sugar and stir until it has dissolved. Bring the mixture to a boil and boil rapidly for 10-15 minutes, or until setting point is reached. With a metal slotted spoon, remove any scum from the surface of the jam.

3 Add the preserved ginger and ginger mint leaves. Pour into sterilized glass jars, seal with waxed paper circles and cover with cellophane lids secured with rubber bands. Decorate with brown paper raffia.

Rose Petal Jelly

This subtle jelly is ideal for polite afternoon teas with thinly sliced pieces of bread and butter – it adds a real summer afternoon flavor to the bread.

ABOUT 2 LB

2½ cups red or pink rose petals

1⁷⁄₈ cups water

generous 3 cups superfine sugar

scant ½ cup bottled white grape juice

scant ½ cup bottled red grape juice

2 oz package powdered fruit pectin

2 tbsp rosewater

1 Trim all the rose petals at the base to remove the white tips. Place the petals, water and about one-eighth of the sugar in a saucepan and bring to a boil. Reduce the heat and simmer for 5 minutes. Remove from the heat and leave to stand overnight for the rose fragrance to infuse.

2 Strain the flowers from the syrup, and put the syrup in a preserving pan or suitable saucepan. Add the grape juices and pectin. Boil hard for 1 minute. Add the rest of the sugar and stir well. Boil the mixture hard for 1 minute more. Remove from the heat.

3 Test for setting – it should make a soft jelly, not a thick jam. Do this by placing a teaspoonful of the hot mixture on a saucer. Leave it to cool: the surface should wrinkle when pushed with a finger. If it is still runny, return the pan to the heat and continue boiling and testing until the jelly sets.

4 Finally add the rosewater. Ladle the jelly into sterilized glass jars and seal with waxed paper circles and cellophane lids secured with rubber bands. Decorate the tops of the jars with circles of fabric held in place with lengths of ribbon.

Cheese and Marjoram Scones

A great success for a hearty tea. With savory toppings, these scones can make a good basis for a light lunch, served with a crunchy, green salad.

ABOUT 18 SCONES

1 cup whole wheat flour

1 cup self-rising flour

pinch salt

scant 3 tbsp butter

¼ tsp dry mustard

2 tsp dried marjoram

½–⅔ cup finely grated sharp Cheddar cheese

1 tsp sunflower oil (optional)

½ cup milk, or as required to make soft dough

⅓ cup pecan nuts or walnuts, chopped

1 Gently sift the two kinds of flour into a bowl and add the salt. Cut the butter into small pieces, and rub these into the flour until it resembles fine breadcrumbs.

2 Add the mustard, marjoram and grated cheese, and mix in sufficient milk to make a soft dough. Knead the dough lightly.

3 Preheat the oven to 425°F. Roll out the dough on a floured surface to about ¾ in thickness and cut it out with a 2 in square cutter. Grease some cookie sheets with the paper from the butter (or use a little sunflower oil), and place the scones on the sheets.

4 Brush the scones with a little milk and sprinkle the chopped pecans or walnuts over the top. Bake for 12 minutes. Serve warm.

Dill and Potato Cakes

Potato cakes are quite scrumptious and should be more widely made. Try this spendid combination and you are sure to be converted.

ABOUT 10 CAKES

2 cups self-rising flour

3 tbsp butter, softened

pinch of salt

1 tbsp finely chopped fresh dill

scant 1 cup mashed potato,
  freshly made

2-3 tbsp milk, as required

1 Preheat the oven to 450°F. Sift the flour into a bowl, and add the butter, salt and dill. Mix in the mashed potato and enough milk to make a soft, pliable dough.

2 Roll out the dough on a well-floured surface until it is fairly thin. Cut into several neat rounds with a 3 in cutter.

3 Grease a cookie sheet, place the cakes on it, and bake for 20-25 minutes until risen and golden.

Rosemary Bread

Sliced thinly, this herb bread is delicious with cheese or soup for a light meal.

1 LOAF

1 x ¼ oz package dried fast-action yeast

1½ cups whole wheat flour

1½ cups self-rising flour

2 tbsp butter, plus more to grease bowl and pan

¼ cup warm water (110°F)

1 cup milk, whole or 2% (room temperature)

1 tbsp sugar

1 tsp salt

1 tbsp sesame seeds

1 tbsp dried chopped onion

1 tbsp fresh rosemary leaves, plus more to decorate

1 cup cubed Cheddar cheese

coarse salt, to decorate

1 Mix the fast-action yeast with the flours in a large mixing bowl. Melt the butter. Stir in the warm water, milk, sugar, butter, salt, sesame seeds, onion and rosemary. Knead thoroughly until quite smooth.

2 Flatten the dough, then add the cheese cubes. Quickly knead them in until they have been well combined.

3 Place the dough into a clean bowl greased with a little butter, turning it so that it becomes greased on all sides. Cover with a clean, dry cloth. Put the greased bowl and dough in a warm place for about 1½ hours, or until the dough has risen and doubled in size.

4 Grease a 9 x 5 in loaf pan with the remaining butter. Knock down the dough to remove some of the air, and shape it into a loaf. Put the loaf into the pan, cover with the clean cloth used earlier and leave for about 1 hour until doubled in size once again. Preheat the oven to 375°F.

5 Bake for 30 minutes. During the last 5-10 minutes of baking, cover the loaf with foil to prevent it from becoming too dark. Remove from the loaf pan and leave to cool on a wire rack. Decorate with rosemary leaves and coarse salt scattered on top.

Blackberry, Sloe Gin and Rosewater Muffins

Other berries can be substituted for the blackberries, such as elderberries or blueberries.

2½ cups plain unbleached flour

generous ¼ cup light brown sugar

4 tsp baking powder

pinch of salt

generous ½ cup chopped blanched almonds

generous ½ cup fresh blackberries

2 eggs

⅞ cup milk

4 tbsp melted butter, plus a little more to grease cups, if using

1 tbsp sloe gin

1 tbsp rosewater

1 Mix the flour, sugar, baking powder and salt in a bowl and gently stir in the almonds and blackberries, mixing them well to coat with the flour mixture. Preheat the oven to 400°F.

2 In another bowl, mix the eggs with the milk, then gradually add the butter, sloe gin and rosewater. Make a well in the center of the bowl of dry ingredients and add the egg and milk mixture. Stir well.

3 Spoon the mixture into greased muffin cups or cases. Bake for 20-25 minutes or until browned. Turn out the muffins on to a wire rack to cool. Serve with butter.

Chocolate and Mint Fudge Cake

Chocolate and mint are popular partners and they blend well in this unusual recipe. The French have been using potato flour in cakes for years. Mashed potato works just as well.

1 CAKE

6-10 fresh mint leaves

³/₄ cup superfine sugar

½ cup butter, plus extra to grease pan

½ cup freshly made mashed potato

2 oz semi-sweet chocolate, melted

1½ cups self-rising flour

pinch of salt

2 eggs, beaten

FILLING

4 fresh mint leaves

½ cup butter

⁷/₈ cup confectioners' sugar

2 tbsp chocolate mint liqueur

TOPPING

1 cup butter

¼ cup granulated sugar

2 tbsp chocolate mint liqueur

2 tbsp water

1½ cups confectioners' sugar

¼ cup cocoa powder

pecan halves, to decorate

1 Tear the mint leaves into small pieces and mix with the superfine sugar. Leave overnight. When you use the flavored sugar, remove the leaves and discard them.

Opposite: *Chocolate and Mint Fudge Cake; Strawberry Mint Sponge*

2 Preheat the oven to 400°F. Cream the butter and sugar with the mashed potato, then add the melted chocolate. Sift in half the flour with a pinch of salt and add half of the beaten eggs. Mix well, then add the remaining flour and the eggs.

3 Grease and line an 8 in pan and pile in the mixture. Bake for 25-30 minutes or until a skewer or pointed knife stuck into the center comes away clean. Turn out on to a wire rack to cool. When cool, split into two layers.

4 Chop the mint leaves in a food processor, then add the butter and sugar. Once the cake is cool, sprinkle the chocolate mint liqueur over both halves and sandwich together with the filling.

5 Put the butter, granulated sugar, liqueur and water into a small pan. Melt the butter and sugar, then boil for 5 minutes. Sieve the confectioners' sugar and cocoa and add the butter and liqueur mixture. Beat until cool and thick. Cover the cake with this mixture, and decorate with the pecan halves.

Strawberry Mint Cake

This combination of fruit, mint and ice cream is a real winner.

1 CAKE

6-10 fresh mint leaves, plus more to decorate

³/₄ cup superfine sugar

³/₄ cup butter, plus extra to grease pan

3 eggs

1½ cups self-rising flour

2½ pints strawberry ice cream

2½ cups heavy cream

2 tbsp mint liqueur

2 cups fresh strawberries

1 Tear the mint into pieces and mix with the superfine sugar. Leave overnight.

2 Grease and line a deep springform cake pan. Preheat the oven to 375°F. Remove the mint from the sugar. Mix the butter and sugar together and add the flour, then the eggs. Pile the mixture into the pan.

3 Bake for 20-25 minutes, or until a skewer or pointed knife inserted in the middle comes away clean. Turn out on to a wire rack to cool. When cool, carefully split horizontally into two equal halves.

4 Clean the cake pan and line it with plastic wrap. Put the bottom half of the cake back in the pan. Spread on the ice cream mixture and level the top. Put on the top half of the cake and freeze for 3-4 hours.

5 Whip the cream with the mint liqueur. Remove the cake from the freezer and quickly spread a layer of whipped cream all over it, leaving a rough finish. Put the cake back into the freezer until about 10 minutes before serving. Decorate the cake with the strawberries and place fresh mint leaves on the plate around the cake.

Carrot Cake with Geranium Cheese

At a pinch you can justify carrot cake as being good for you – at least this is an excuse for taking a good many calories on board. But the flavor is definitely worth it.

1 CAKE

2-3 scented geranium leaves
  (preferably with a lemon scent)
2 cups icing sugar
1 cup self-rising flour
1 tsp baking of soda
½ tsp ground cinnamon
½ tsp ground cloves
1 cup brown sugar
1½ cups grated carrot
½ cup sultanas
½ cup finely chopped preserved
  ginger
½ cup pecan nuts
⅔ cup sunflower oil
2 eggs, lightly beaten
butter to grease tin
CREAM CHEESE TOPPING
generous ¼ cup cream cheese
2 tbsp softened butter
1 tsp grated lemon rind

1 Put the geranium leaves, torn into small- to medium-sized pieces, in a small bowl and mix with the confectioners' sugar. Leave in a warm place overnight for the sugar to take up the scent of the leaves.

From left: *Lavender Cookies; Carrot Cake with Geranium Cheese*

2 Sift the flour, soda and spices together. Add the soft brown sugar, carrots, sultanas, ginger and pecans. Stir well then add the oil and beaten eggs. Mix with an electric beater for about 5 minutes, or 10-15 minutes longer by hand.

3 Preheat the oven to 350°F. Grease a 5 x 9 in loaf pan, line the base with waxed paper, and then grease the paper. Pour the mixture into the pan and bake for about 1 hour. Remove the cake from the oven, leave to stand for a few minutes, and then turn it out on to a wire rack until completely cool.

4 While the cake is cooling, make the cream cheese topping. Remove the pieces of geranium leaf from the confectioners' sugar and discard them. Place the cream cheese, butter and lemon rind in a bowl. Using an electric beater or a wire whisk, gradually add the confectioners' sugar, beating well until smooth.

5 Once the cake has cooled, cover the top with the cream cheese mixture.

Lavender Cookies

Instead of lavender you can use any other flavoring, such as cinnamon, lemon, orange or mint.

ABOUT 30

⅝ cup butter, plus more to grease
  baking sheets
½ cup granulated sugar
1 egg, beaten
1 tbsp dried lavender flowers
1½ cups self-rising flour
assorted leaves and flowers,
  to decorate

1 Preheat the oven to 350°F. Cream the butter and sugar together, then stir in the egg. Mix in the lavender flowers and the flour.

2 Grease two cookie sheets and drop spoonfuls of the mixture on them. Bake for about 15-20 minutes, until the cookies are golden. Serve with some fresh leaves and flowers to decorate.

Herb-Decorated Crackers

Home-made touches are important at Christmas, as they add the final touch to a family celebration. These crackers are easy to decorate and could be made by adults and children together. Buy ready-decorated crackers and remove the commercial trimming.

crackers
narrow ribbon, as preferred
scissors
small sprigs of various herbs, as
  preferred
hot glue gun, or general-purpose
  adhesive

1 Tie the ends of the crackers with ribbon, making attractive bows.

2 Make small posies of herbs and glue them to the middle part of the crackers.

Scented Pressed Herb Diary

 *A notebook or diary can be scented by placing it in a box with a strong lavender sachet, or a cotton-wool ball sprinkled with a few drops of essential oil. Leave it in the sealed box for a month or so to impart a sweet lingering fragrance. Another idea is to wipe the inside of the covers lightly with a small amount of essential oil on a lint pad. Try to find a very plain diary or notebook which does not have lettering or decoration on the cover, as these would spoil the design. Use a plastic film made for covering books. Some types are ironed on, others cling by themselves.*

pressed leaves and flowers, such as borage flowers, alchemilla flowers and small leaves, daisies, single roses, forget-me-nots
plain diary or notebook
tweezers
large tapestry needle
rubber cement
clear plastic film
iron and cloth pad, if required

1 Start by arranging a selection of pressed leaves on the front of the diary or notebook, using the tweezers for positioning.

2 Continue to build up your design by adding the pressed flower heads.

3 Once you are happy with the design stick it down, using a large tapestry needle and rubber cement. Slide the needle into the glue and then, without moving the design, place a small amount of glue under each leaf and petal so that they are secure. Cover with clear film. If the film needs heating, iron gently with a cloth pad between the film and the iron.

Pressed Herb Cards

 *A home-made card is always one that will be treasured long after the occasion has passed. Although it takes time and trouble to make your own cards, you could make a batch and keep them for a suitable occasion. It is always worth the effort to give someone something with your personal touch.*

pressed herbs and flowers, such as blue cornflower, ivy, rosemary, borage
blank greeting card
large tapestry needle
rubber cement
clear plastic film
iron and cloth pad, if required

1 Arrange a selection of pressed herbs and flowers on the front of the card, using tweezers for positioning.

2 When the design is complete, stick it down, using a large tapestry needle and rubber cement. Using the needle, slide small dabs of adhesive beneath the herbs and flowers without altering their position. Cover with a clear film. If the film needs heating, iron gently with a cloth pad between the film and the iron.

Right: *assorted Pressed Herb Cards and Scented Pressed Herb Diaries*

Chamomile and Honey Mask

Although this mask makes you look a little strange while it is on your face, it smooths and softens skin beautifully. Chamomile flowers are usually easy to obtain from a health food shop as they are often used for making chamomile tea.

1 tbsp dried chamomile flowers
¾ cup boiling water
2 tbsp bran
1 tsp clear honey, warmed

1 Pour the boiling water over the chamomile flowers and allow them to stand for 30 minutes. Then strain the infusion and discard the chamomile flowers.

2 Mix 3 tbsp of the liquid with the bran and honey and rub this mixture all over your face. It may be a little stiff at first but will smooth out over the skin. Leave the mixture on your skin for at least 10 minutes, then rinse off with warm water.

Stockists and Suppliers

HERB SEEDS AND PLANTS

Cameron Park Botanicals
Highway 64 East
Raleigh, NC 27610
(Newsletter; catalogue available)

Caprilands Herb Farm
Silver Street
North Coventry. CT 06238

Flag Fork Herb Farm
260 Flag Fork Road
Frankfurt, KY 40601
(Catalog available)

The HerbFarm
32804 Issaquah-Fall City Road
Fall City, IA 98024
(206) 784 2222
(Catalog: $3.50)

Richter's Herb Catalogue
Goodwood
Ontario,
Canada, LOC 1A0
(416) 640 6677
(Catalog: $2.00 US and Canadian)

Seeds Blum
Idaho City Stage
Boise, ID 83706
Fax (208) 338 5658
(Catalog: $3.00)

Taylor's Herb Gardens
1535 Lone Oak Road
Vista, CA 92084
(691) 727 3485
(Catalog: $3.00)

POTPOURRI. BLENDED AND ESSENTIAL OILS SUPPLIES

Bonny Doon Farm
600 Marin Road
Santa Cruz, CA 95060
(Catalog available)

Hanna's Potpourri
Specialties Inc.
P.O. Box 3647
Fayetteville, AK 72702
(800) 327 9826

Herb Garden Fragrances
3744 Section Road
Cincinnati, OH 45236

Kiehl's
109 Third Avenue
New York, NY 10003

Lorann Oils
4518 Aurelius Road
P.O. Box 22009
Lansing, MI 48909-2009
(800) 248 1302

Mrs. O'Quinn's Scent Shoppe
1908 Joanne Street
Wichita, KS 67203

Picture Acknowledgements
All photographs in this book were taken by John Freeman and Michelle Garrett, apart from those on pages 36 (left) and 37, 54 and 55 and pages 36 (right), 75 (hollyhocks), 77 (sea thrift), 81 (knapweed), 82 (chamomile), 87 (rocket), 90 (herb robert), 93 (woad), 95 (lavender), 98 (mallow), 107 (greater plantain), 113 (savory) and 117 (variegated Russian comfrey) which were kindly lent by Jenny Balfour-Paul, Jacqui Hurst and the Garden Picture Library respectively. The pictures on pages 7 (bottom), 8 (top and bottom left) and 9 (right) were lent by Visual Arts Library.